# Tiny Habits That Create Changes

## Discover The Best Small Changes That Will Boost Your Productivity

**Dr. James K. Fogg**

# Table Of Contents

# Dedication

To all the dreamers who dare to start small but think big—this book is for you.

To the countless individuals who wrestle with change, persist through setbacks, and believe in the quiet power of tiny steps taken every day—your courage inspires every page.

To my family and friends, whose unwavering support and patience have been the bedrock beneath this journey.

And to the teachers, mentors, and kindred spirits, near and far, who have shared wisdom and light along the winding path of growth—this work honors your gifts.

May this book serve as a companion and catalyst, reminding you that transformation lives not in sudden leaps but in gentle, persistent footprints laid steadily toward a life well-lived.

# Introduction

Habits are powerful forces shaping our daily lives—often without our notice. From the moment we wake until we sleep, countless actions happen automatically: the cup of coffee poured without thought, the phone checked reflexively, or the drive to work executed without conscious navigation. These ingrained routines, collectively called habits, are the invisible threads weaving the fabric of who we are.

Understanding habits' nature and their profound impact is the first crucial step on the path to meaningful change. Habits are not merely behaviors but mental shortcuts the brain creates to conserve energy and improve efficiency. Neuroscience reveals that nearly half of our actions each day emerge from these automatic loops, formed through repeated cues, behaviors, and rewards.

Consider Anna, a young professional struggling with productivity and self-doubt. Despite her ambitions, she found herself trapped in cycles of procrastination. However, when Anna began identifying her habits—recognizing how a stress cue led her to check social media and how this provided a fleeting reward—she realized her behaviors were not random but systematic. This insight empowered her to tweak her environment, replace routines, and develop habits aligned with her goals. Slowly, Anna transformed her workflow and reclaimed control over her time.

Habits impact far beyond simple tasks. They fundamentally shape our health, relationships, mindset, and career trajectory. Positive habits—such as regular exercise, mindful communication, and effective planning—compound to yield enhanced well-being and success. Negative habits, conversely, create cycles that hinder growth and cause distress.

Science confirms habits' durability stems from neural pathways in the brain's basal ganglia, which encode routines, making them efficient but also resistant to conscious change. Yet, this same system enables adaptation; with awareness and practice, new habits can rewire these pathways.

This book invites you to explore how habits work and how to harness their power. With personal stories like Anna's, combined with scientific insight, you will learn to cultivate habits that support lasting change—not through willpower alone, but through designing your daily life intentionally.

Your journey starts with understanding these unseen drivers of behavior to create a future shaped by your conscious choices, one habit at a time.

## Why changing habits is challenging

Changing habits can feel like trying to rewrite the inner workings of your mind—an endeavor that often feels overwhelming and fraught with setbacks. This challenge arises from how deeply habits are woven into our brains and daily lives.

At its core, habit change requires interrupting established neurological pathways created by repeated behavior over time. The basal ganglia, a brain area specialized in running habitual routines automatically, makes these patterns energy-efficient but resistant to conscious change. This resistance means that even with strong intentions, old habits often assert themselves, especially under stress or fatigue when mental resources wane.

Moreover, habits are tightly linked to cues embedded in our environment and emotional states. These triggers are often subtle, making self-regulation difficult without keen awareness. Removing or replacing a habit involves not just stopping a behavior but managing the web of cues and emotional responses that sustain it.

Willpower and motivation, though often relied upon, are finite and fluctuate daily. Approaches focusing solely on sheer determination tend to falter because they demand sustained high effort against ingrained neural circuits.

## Maya's Journey Through Habit Change

Maya faced years of struggle with emotional eating. She resolved repeatedly to eat healthily but found herself falling back into old patterns triggered by stress and loneliness. Initially, she aimed for comprehensive diet overhauls, which led to burnout.

Her breakthrough came when she shifted focus to tiny habits. Instead of transforming everything overnight, Maya began with the small step of drinking a glass of water before each meal. This tiny habit was easy to accomplish and provided a new cue-routine-reward loop that began breaking her automatic overeating.

With patience and consistent tiny steps, Maya gradually built new, healthier habits that aligned with her emotional needs and lifestyle. Her story shows that while habit change is hard, tiny, manageable actions can yield powerful, lasting transformation.

## Importance of Tiny Habits for Lasting Change

Tiny habits—the concept of adopting small, easily achievable behaviors—leverage how the brain naturally forms habits. These mini behaviors lower the "activation energy" needed to start, reducing resistance and increasing the likelihood of consistency.

Unlike sweeping life changes, tiny habits:

Fit effortlessly into daily life without overwhelming motivation or willpower

Build positive feedback loops that increase internal rewards and reinforce behavior

Create momentum, where one small habit primes other positive actions

Are adaptable to varying circumstances, sustaining habit growth even during challenges

The science of neuroplasticity—the brain's ability to rewire itself—underscores the benefits of tiny habits. Repetitive small behaviors create and strengthen neural pathways over time, gradually automating desired changes without triggering the brain's resistance.

## Practical Example: The Power of Tiny Habits in Action

James wanted to improve his physical activity. Instead of aiming for an hour-long workout immediately, he chose a tiny habit: putting on his running shoes right after brushing his teeth. This small cue triggered the routine and built momentum.

With time, this modest act led James to longer runs and consistent exercise. The tiny habit minimized friction, boosted his confidence, and enabled sustainable change by aligning with the brain's natural learning process.

## Why Tiny Habits Work Better Than Big Resolutions

Big resolutions often fail because they set high bars and external pressure, which can quickly erode motivation. Tiny habits sidestep this by emphasizing progress over perfection, focusing on ease and reward.

They foster **identity change**, where consistent small wins help reframe how you see yourself ("I am someone who takes care of my health") rather than controlling behavior through obligation alone.

Changing habits is inherently challenging due to deeply embedded neural wiring and environmental and emotional cues. However, embracing tiny habits offers a science-backed, compassionate pathway to lasting change.

Maya and James' stories highlight that sustainable transformation comes not from heroic effort but accumulated small steps, each activating new neural patterns and reinforcing positive identity.

## How this book will help boost your productivity

In today's world, productivity is often seen as the ultimate key to success, fulfillment, and happiness. Yet many of us find ourselves caught in cycles of distraction, burnout, and overwhelm, struggling to get the important work done. The truth is, boosting productivity isn't just about working harder or longer—it's about working smarter by understanding and harnessing the powerful role that habits play in shaping our daily effectiveness.

This book focuses on how you can transform your productivity not by willpower alone, but by building small, consistent, and sustainable habits that align with your goals and values. Instead of relying on motivation—which fluctuates—or pushing through exhaustion, you'll learn how to optimize your brain's natural tendencies, automate positive behaviors, and design a system that supports continuous growth with less struggle.

## The Core Promise: Building a Habit-Based Productivity System

You might wonder: How exactly can habits boost productivity? The answer lies in the science of how habits automate action and conserve mental resources. When important tasks become habitual, your brain no longer needs to expend excessive energy deciding whether or how to do them. This reduces decision fatigue and allows your focus, creativity, and energy to be channeled into higher-level work that requires conscious problem-solving.

Throughout this book, you will discover how to:

- Identify existing habits that either help or hinder your productivity

- Design new habits that foster consistency, focus, and energy management

- Break down overwhelming goals into tiny, manageable actions that build momentum

- Anticipate and overcome common productivity pitfalls such as procrastination and burnout

Leverage the power of rewards and cues to reinforce positive behavioral loops

Customize your environment and routines to naturally support your best work

## Alex's Transformation from Overwhelm to Flow

Alex was once caught in a relentless cycle of endless to-do lists and scattered focus. He worked late nights, jumping between tasks, only to feel increasingly exhausted and unfulfilled. The harder he pushed, the deeper he sank into distraction and burnout.

One pivotal day, Alex decided to create a habit of a five-minute morning planning ritual. It was a tiny commitment but one that brought clarity, grounding his day's work around priorities rather than urgency. Each morning, the habit set the tone for a focused, productive day.

Over weeks, Alex built upon this simple habit. He added short breaks every hour and a nightly reflection practice. Fragmented actions solidified into a seamless, habit-driven system. Productivity no longer felt like a battle but a flowing, manageable rhythm.

Alex's journey illustrates that productivity flourishes not from perfection or quantity but from strategically built habits that conserve effort and promote consistency.

## Meeting You Where You Are

No matter your current productivity level, lifestyle demands, or personality, this book offers adaptable insights and exercises. Whether you are a freelancer struggling with discipline, a manager juggling meetings, or a student overwhelmed with studying, you will find tools that match your context and challenges.

By emphasizing incremental change grounded in habit science, you'll reduce overwhelm and set yourself up for success even during seasons of unpredictability or low motivation.

## Practical Value: From Science to Daily Practice

Understanding brain science alone isn't enough—translating it into practical action is vital. This book bridges that gap by pairing research with actionable strategies and relatable stories to make complex ideas accessible and applicable.

You will learn how to harness the habit loop (cue, routine, reward) to automate productivity behaviors, avoid common traps, and flexibly adapt your system as your goals evolve.

## The Long-Term Vision: Sustainable, Joyful Productivity

Ultimately, the goal is not just to get more done but to create a joyful, sustainable way of working aligned with what matters most to you. This frame shifts productivity from a source of stress to a source of empowerment.

As you cultivate habits that support focus, energy, and well-being, productivity becomes less of a distant aspiration and more of an experienced reality—one that enriches your work, life, and sense of fulfillment.

This book is a guide, a companion, and a toolkit for your unique productivity journey. Like Alex, you can move from chaos to clarity, from burnout to balance, by embracing the power of tiny, consistent habits.

Your path to productivity transformation begins here—with understanding, compassion for yourself, and an actionable plan rooted in the science of habits. Step by step, habit by habit, you will build a life of focus, flow, and meaningful achievement.

# Chapter One

## The Power of Tiny Habits

### Why tiny habits require less motivation

Change is often misunderstood as a monumental task that hinges solely on motivation and willpower. The truth, however, is that motivation is an unreliable and often fleeting resource. That's where tiny habits come in—they are the secret allies of lasting transformation, requiring remarkably less motivation to form and sustain.

The human brain is wired to conserve energy. Because of this, our neural architecture tends to resist efforts demanding high mental or physical exertion. Large-scale behavioral changes, although inspiring in theory, often trigger mental resistance because they clash with the brain's preference for efficiency. This resistance manifests as procrastination, self-doubt, and abandonment of goals.

Tiny habits neatly sidestep this barrier. By definition, they are small, manageable actions that are easy to start and maintain. The sheer simplicity lowers the activation energy needed—meaning that the brain doesn't fight against these behaviors as much as larger, more complex ones. This ease translates directly into sustained momentum and progressive change.

## Understanding the Brain's Energy Economy

Your brain burns about 20% of your body's energy but seeks to minimize unnecessary expenditure. Habit formation is an energy-saving mechanism where repeated behaviors become neurologically hardwired, allowing them to run automatically with minimal conscious effort.

Large habits demand high cognitive engagement initially and often invoke the activity of the prefrontal cortex, the brain's decision center. Tiny habits, in contrast, capitalize on existing routines or natural cues to create minimal disruptions. They harness the basal ganglia's capacity to automate behaviors, making the transition from conscious effort to effortless repetition faster and smoother.

## Carlos' Small Step Toward Overcoming Procrastination

Carlos was a talent stuck in a cycle of procrastination. He intended to write regularly but was often overwhelmed by the idea of producing entire drafts in one sitting. His motivation would spike and crash, leading to bouts of guilt and frustration.

One day, Carlos decided to write just a single sentence after his morning coffee rather than an entire page. This tiny habit, rooted in his existing routine, required almost no motivation. Surprisingly, it sparked a new rhythm. Within weeks, he naturally expanded from one sentence to multiple paragraphs.

Carlos' journey reveals how the perceived Herculean task of habit change becomes overwhelmingly manageable when broken into tiny chunks. His initial success reduced mental barriers and fueled his confidence, showing how tiny habits bypass the motivation hurdle.

## Why Motivation Fluctuates and Why Tiny Habits Persist

Motivation is subject to many internal and external factors—from mood and energy to environment and stress. This variability makes forming large new habits precarious. When motivation wanes, temptation to abandon big efforts rises.

Tiny habits, however, minimize reliance on motivation by reducing the effort threshold. A habit as small as "do one push-up daily" feels feasible regardless of motivation, allowing you to stay consistent even during low-energy periods. This consistency, built on ease, carves out a foundation for momentum that fuels bigger change.

## The Psychological Safety of Tiny Wins

When you accomplish something—even tiny—you trigger positive emotions associated with success. These emotions reinforce habit loops and build identity shifts ("I am someone who does this?"). Large goals often fail because they expose us to failure and feelings of inadequacy, while tiny habits create frequent "wins" that sustain motivation over time.

## Practical Tips for Leveraging Tiny Habits

**Anchor to an existing habit or time:** Link the tiny action to something already habitual (e.g., "After I pour my morning coffee, I will stand and stretch.")

**Keep it ridiculously simple:** If it feels like a chore, it's too big. Shrink until it's almost effortless.

**Celebrate immediately:** A small gesture, like smiling or saying "Good job," increases dopamine and solidifies the routine.

**Allow flexibility:** Some days, doing the habit takes seconds; other days, naturally more. The key is acting consistently, not perfectly.

## Embrace the Small to Achieve the Big

Tiny habits represent a profound shift in how we approach change. They honor the brain's natural wiring, reduce psychological resistance, and build momentum through achievable consistency rather than heroic effort.

Carlos' journey demonstrates that by starting small, even the most daunting behaviors become accessible. Motivation is no longer the master but the companion, supported by the structure of tiny, sustainable habits.

This part of the chapter equips you with the understanding and encouragement to welcome change gently, cultivating the power of tiny habits for lasting success.

## The Safety and Sustainability of Tiny Habits

Change can feel risky, intimidating, and unsustainable—especially when past attempts have ended in burnout or frustration. Huge goals and radical lifestyle shifts often bring unintended consequences such as guilt, stress, or failure.

Tiny habits provide a safer, more sustainable route to transformation. They align with human psychology and brain function, enabling growth that preserves well-being and self-compassion.

## Why Safety Matters in Habit Change

The concept of safety here is twofold:

**Psychological safety:** Creating habits that protect self-esteem and reduce fear of failure.

**Physical safety:** Ensuring habits don't cause harm or strain to the body.

Many large-scale habit changes crush motivation because they overwhelm mental and physical capacities. Tiny habits mitigate this risk by respecting your current limits.

## Minimal Risk of Overwhelm and Burnout

Tiny habits avoid overload by being intentionally small. This prevents the exhaustion often caused by drastic new routines. For example, someone aiming to exercise for an hour daily may find motivation waning and body fatigued, while the habit of doing one push-up after waking poses virtually no drain but still seeds growth.

Tiny habits reduce the likelihood of burnout because they:

Demand minimal effort

Fit naturally into existing routines

Foster positive reinforcement without pressure

This nurturing approach encourages gradual progress without sacrificing mental health.

## Maya's Compassionate Habit Journey

Maya had struggled with cycles of intense dieting and guilt-fueled binges. Each attempt at big change left her disheartened and fearful of failure.

In her journey towards wellness, Maya embraced tiny habits like taking a single mindful breath before meals or standing for two minutes after work. These gentle shifts didn't intimidate her or demand immense willpower.

Over time, these safe, nonjudgmental habits built her confidence and reconnected her body and mind with kindness rather than punishment. Maya's story shows how safety in habit-building fosters sustained change rooted in compassion.

## The Sustainability of Tiny Habits: Building on Small Wins

Sustainability means a habit endures long term, integrating seamlessly without friction. Tiny habits build sustainability by capitalizing on small wins that accumulate.

Each tiny habit practiced consistently leads to strengthened neural pathways through neuroplasticity, converting voluntary action into automatic behavior. This neural efficiency means habits require less effort over time, enhancing adherence.

## Flexibility and Adaptability

Life is dynamic. Tiny habits are resilient because they accommodate fluctuations in energy, mood, and environment. On busy or challenging days, a tiny habit can still be completed. On easier days, they naturally expand.

For instance, a tiny habit of five minutes of reading can grow into a full chapter, or pause at just a paragraph if time is short. This adaptability fosters consistency and prevents all-or-nothing thinking that undermines persistence.

## Avoiding the Trap of Perfectionism

Tiny habits combat the perfectionism trap by setting low, achievable goals. This reduces feelings of failure and guilt. Failure to stick to a huge goal often results in abandoning change altogether, while tiny habits invite repeated practice with no penalty for variability.

## Practical Tools to Enhance Safety and Sustainability

Anchor habits to existing behaviors to ensure seamless integration.

Track tiny habit completions to visualize progress and build motivation.

Celebrate small wins to enhance reward pathways.

Modify or shrink habits as needed—progress over perfection is key.

## David's Sustainable Career Shift

David was overwhelmed when he decided to re-skill for a career change. Massive study plans caused anxiety and inconsistency.

He shifted to tiny habits—studying one page daily, researching one helpful article, or spending two minutes organizing his workspace. This manageable approach kept burnout at bay and made learning joyful.

David's sustainable habit-building transformed daunting goals into achievable daily success, illustrating how small changes endure when safe and adaptable.

Tiny habits embody safety and sustainability in behavior change, respecting your limits and fostering enduring progress. They minimize risks of burnout and failure, encouraging growth through kindness and adaptability.

Maya and David's journeys teach that transformation need not be harsh or overwhelming. Safe, tiny habits create fertile soil where lasting success grows with resilience and joy.

## Treating Habits as a System for Behavior Change

Many people view habits as isolated actions—simple behaviors to start or stop. Yet this fragmented perspective limits the potential for meaningful, lasting change. Real transformation emerges when you understand habits as interconnected parts of a dynamic system influencing all areas of life.

Treating habits as a system means seeing how individual behaviors interact, how environments, cues, routines, and rewards shape these behaviors, and how they collectively create your identity, health, and productivity.

This systems approach offers a roadmap to design deliberate, powerful, and sustainable behavior change that transcends mere willpower and motivation.

## The Concept of Habit Systems

A habit system is an organized network of behaviors that operate together to produce outcomes. Think of it as a web where each habit supports or shapes the others.

For example, a morning routine system might include waking up at a specific time, drinking water, light exercise, and journaling, all reinforcing each other and contributing to well-being. Neglecting one part often weakens the entire system.

Recognizing the systemic nature of habits empowers you to manage and improve behavior holistically rather than piecemeal.

## Advantages of Systemic Habit Change

**Cumulative Impact:** Small changes within a system multiply their effects, amplifying results beyond individual habit gains.

**Resilience and Flexibility:** Systems can absorb disruptions in one part without total breakdown, enabling sustained change amid life's unpredictability.

**Identity Reinforcement:** Systems cultivate a self-concept aligned with desired outcomes, with behaviors supporting your sense of who you are.

**Holistic Success:** Progress in one domain (like sleep) positively influences others (like focus and mood), creating synergy.

## Rachel's Integrated System for Well-being

Rachel, a graphic designer and mother, struggled to balance work stresses with family demands, frequently feeling burned out.

She initially tried changing isolated habits—like exercising or eating better—but progress was erratic. After learning about habit systems, Rachel designed a holistic daily framework:

> Morning hydration and meditation to center herself.

> Dedicated focused work blocks with planned breaks.

> Evening family time and reading rituals.

> Journaling reflections to track moods and progress.

This system interconnected habits, each cueing and supporting others, forming a flow that became self-sustaining.

Disruptions like overtime workdays caused less upheaval because the system's other parts held steady. Rachel's identity shifted from overwhelmed to resilient and balanced.

Her story illustrates how habit systems cultivate deeper, sustained change.

## Designing Your Habit System: Practical Steps

**Map Your Current Behaviors:** Identify key habits shaping your days, noting how they connect and areas needing improvement.

**Define Desired Outcomes:** Clarify what successful change looks like in your life.

**Build Interlinked Habits:** Create habits that cue and support each other, starting tiny and scalable.

**Optimize Environment:** Arrange your surroundings to reinforce cues and reduce friction.

**Track and Adjust:** Monitor system performance and adapt as life shifts.

## Systems Thinking Enhances Motivation and Willpower

By viewing habits as a system, motivation shifts from overwhelming artifice to natural flow. The system's momentum carries you, reducing reliance on sporadic willpower.

Consistency grows from systemic interconnections rather than isolated effort bursts.

## Practical Example: Sophia's Productivity System

Sophia, a freelance writer, struggled with fragmented productivity. Through a habit system approach, she developed:

> A fixed morning routine anchoring focus rituals.

> Time-blocking habits for work and rest.

> Mini-break mindfulness practices.

> Nightly review to reinforce learning and success.

This interconnected system transformed scattered days into productive flows, vastly improving results and well-being.

Treating habits as a system revolutionizes behavior change. It offers sustainable, adaptable, and identity-shaping growth beyond isolated habits.

Rachel and Sophia's stories exemplify the profound power of systemic habits to create resilient, lifelong transformation.

As you continue your journey, remember that designing your unique habit system harnesses the complexity of behavior for your success.

# Chapter Two

## The Science of Habit Formation

### The Habit Loop: Cue, Routine, Reward

Habits are the invisible architecture of our daily lives. They shape who we are and how we live, often without us even realizing it. At the heart of habit formation lies a simple but powerful process called the habit loop, which consists of three key components: the cue, the routine, and the reward. Understanding this loop is the first step to mastering habits—to breaking destructive ones or building empowering new ones.

### Understanding the Habit Loop

The habit loop is like a circle of influence driving our behavior. It begins when the brain receives a cue or trigger—something that tells it to initiate a certain behavior. This leads to the routine—the action or behavior itself. Finally, there is the reward, which satisfies a craving or need, reinforcing the behavior and planting the seed for the habit to repeat.

> **Cue**: This is the spark that starts the habit. It could be a time of day, an emotional state, a location, or even a person. The cue tells your brain, "It's time to do this."

> **Routine**: This is the actual behavior or action you perform. It can be physical, mental, or emotional.

> **Reward**: This is what your brain gets out of the routine, the satisfying payoff that tells your mind, "That was worth it." The reward helps the brain remember the habit loop and encourages it to repeat next time the cue appears.

By realizing how these three components interact, you can bring conscious control over habits instead of being their victim.

## Breaking Free from the Morning Slump

When I first met Sarah, she shared how every morning was a struggle. Without fail, the moment her alarm went off, she'd hit snooze repeatedly. The cue—the sound of the alarm—triggered an overwhelming desire to stay in bed (routine). The reward was immediate comfort and relief from the grogginess, even though she knew she'd feel rushed and stressed later.

Sarah felt trapped in this loop for years. But when she began to understand the habit loop, everything changed.

Instead of simply fighting the snooze, she redesigned the cue and reward. She moved her alarm clock across the room, forcing her out of bed to turn it off. This physical movement served as a new cue. Then, to replace the old reward of "just staying comfy," she promised herself a small but satisfying morning treat: a cup of her favorite coffee brewed freshly as soon as she got up.

Over time, her morning routine shifted. The new cue—getting out of bed to silence the alarm—made it easier to break the snooze habit. The routine became standing up and heading to the coffee machine—a small but proactive step. And the reward? The rich taste and aroma of coffee became a positive payoff, creating eagerness to start mornings on a fresh, energized note.

Sarah's story shows how powerful the habit loop is—and how, by tweaking the cue and reward, a whole pattern of behavior can shift.

## The Science Behind the Loop

Research in neuroscience reveals that habits form in a part of the brain called the basal ganglia, which controls emotions, memories, and pattern recognition. When a habit starts, the cue triggers the brain to go on autopilot, following the routine that leads to the reward. The loop enhances efficiency by reducing the need for conscious decision-making, but it also makes habits deeply ingrained.

In a famous experiment, researchers studied a man who had a habit of eating french fries every time he watched TV. The cue was sitting in front of the television, the routine was eating fries, and the reward was the pleasurable taste and distraction from daily stress. Once researchers identified this loop, they helped him replace the routine—when the cue appeared, he snacked on sliced apples instead. The reward (something to crunch on while watching TV) stayed the same, but the routine became healthier.

## Why Understanding the Loop Matters

The good news is that habits can be reshaped. Since the brain follows this loop every time, you only need to change one part to transform your habits. Most often the easiest part to modify is the routine, while keeping the same cue and reward.

Here is how you can start:

**Identify the Cue** — Reflect on what triggers your habit. Is it boredom, stress, a particular time, or a location? The clearer you understand your cues, the more control you gain.

**Change the Routine** — Decide on a healthier or more productive behavior you want to replace the old habit with.

**Keep the Reward** — Ensure the new routine still satisfies the same craving or gives a similar sense of satisfaction.

## John's Battle with Procrastination

John often found himself procrastinating on his work assignments. The cue was feeling overwhelmed by the size of the task, creating anxiety. His routine was to check social media or watch random videos to escape. The reward was temporary relief from stress but led to guilt afterward, creating a destructive loop.

By understanding the habit loop, John made a small but crucial change. He identified his cue—overwhelm—and replaced his escape routine with a five-minute focused work sprint, followed by a reward of a short break or a walk outside. This routine still gave him relief from anxiety (reward) but channeled it productively. Over weeks, his habit loop adjusted, and procrastination lost its grip.

## Simple Tips to Use the Habit Loop for Positive Change

Use visual or physical cues that make the new habit easy to start, like putting workout clothes next to your bed to cue morning exercise.

Attach new routines to existing habits (called "habit stacking"), e.g., after brushing teeth, do five minutes of stretching.

Celebrate small wins as rewards to reinforce the habit emotionally.

Track progress to become more aware of the cues and rewards that control your behavior.

## The Habit Loop in Everyday Life

Think of the habit loop as the programming language of your brain. Just like a computer follows code, your brain follows cue-routine-reward cycles. The more you understand this language, the better you become at rewriting your story.

Whether it's quitting smoking, building a meditation practice, or improving your diet, the habit loop is key. Behind every lasting change is a habit rewired with clear cues, supportive routines, and fulfilling rewards.

The next time you notice a repeated behavior, pause and reflect: What is my cue? What routine do I fall into? What reward am I actually seeking? This simple reflection will give you control. Habits don't just happen; they can be chosen and shaped. The habit loop is your roadmap on that transformative journey.

## How Habits Are Wired in the Brain

At the core of habit formation lies a small but powerful region of the brain called the basal ganglia. This ancient part of the brain is responsible for storing routines and repeated behaviors so that they can be executed automatically, freeing up the rest of the brain for complex thought. When you first learn a new behavior—say, tying your shoelaces or driving a car—it requires intense focus and conscious decision-making. Over time and repetition, the basal ganglia take over, allowing you to perform these tasks without conscious effort.

This shift is the brain's way of increasing efficiency. Imagine if you had to consciously think about every movement every time you brushed your teeth or put on your shoes. Habits save your brain from this overload.

But wiring habits into the brain is not just about repetition. The brain works on a loop of cues, routines, and rewards. It encodes these loops as neural pathways—like trails in a forest. The more often you walk the same path, the clearer and easier it becomes to follow the same route again and again.

There is also a vital part that the prefrontal cortex—the brain's command center—plays in controlling these habits. While the basal ganglia automate repeated actions, the prefrontal cortex decides which habits to allow into your conscious behavior based on context and goals. This insight offers hope that even deeply ingrained habits can be consciously overridden when necessary.

## The Role of Emotions in Habit Formation

If the brain boiled habit formation down to pure mechanics, habits would be machines with no heart. But emotions are the secret sauce that gives habits their power.

Neuroscience shows that dopamine, a chemical messenger in the brain, plays a starring role in habit formation. Dopamine is released when we experience pleasure or satisfaction. This chemical not only makes us feel good but also reinforces the connection between the cue, the routine, and the reward, baking the habit more firmly into our neural circuits.

Put simply: Positive emotions create habits. The feeling you get when fulfilling a habit is what drives your brain to want to repeat it.

This is why some habits form instantly when paired with strong emotions. For example, a teenager given their first smartphone quickly develops a habit of checking it constantly, driven by the excitement and social connection that dopamine releases. The emotional bond makes the habit nearly instantaneous.

On the other hand, emotionally neutral or unpleasant routines are much harder to turn into habits, no matter how much they are repeated. For example, forcing yourself to do a tedious chore becomes difficult to sustain unless you find ways to generate positive emotional associations with it.

## Emma's Coffee Habit and the Power of Emotion

Emma used to struggle with waking up in the mornings. She was a deep sleeper, and the harsh sound of her alarm often triggered irritation and an urge to snooze. But she wanted a better routine—one that started her day energized.

One day, Emma transformed her mornings by attaching a positive emotional reward to her wake-up routine. Instead of rushing out of bed, she prepared her favorite coffee the night before and let its anticipation fill her senses as soon as she woke. The rich aroma and warm first sip brought her a comforting and joyful feeling.

This positive emotional experience—coffee pleasure—became a dopamine release that wired a new habit of waking up early. Her brain started to associate morning wake-up not with irritation but with delight, making it easier to get up without battle.

Emma's story highlights how powerful emotions—especially positive ones—act as the glue that solidifies habits in the brain. When your brain associates a behavior with good feelings, it speeds up forming that habit deeply and permanently.

## The Role of Triggers in Habit Formation

While emotions bind habits with feeling, triggers (or cues) initiate the process.

Triggers are external or internal stimuli that signal the brain, "It's time to start the routine now." These can take many forms:

**Time cues:** Specific times of day (7 am wake-up)

**Location cues:** Entering a particular place (walking into the gym)

**Emotional states:** Feeling stressed, bored, or happy

**Preceding actions:** Finishing a meal (brush teeth after)

**Social environment:** Seeing friends (prompting greetings or behaviors)

Triggers are powerful because they prompt your brain to switch from conscious control to autopilot, immediately starting the learned routine.

The challenge comes when triggers are associated with unwanted habits. For example, feeling stressed might trigger nail-biting or smoking. Every time stress appears, the brain goes straight into the habit routine to find quick relief.

Understanding and controlling triggers is a cornerstone of habit change. Either you avoid triggers connected to bad habits or consciously associate new, positive routines to the same triggers.

## Mark's Battle with Stress Eating

Mark knew he was a stress eater. After long, pressure-filled days at work, he could never resist reaching for junk food even though he felt guilty afterward. He realized that his emotional state—stress—acted as a trigger for a habit he wanted to break.

Instead of trying to suppress the urge, Mark worked on recognizing his stress as the trigger. He then created a new routine to respond: a brief mindfulness breathing exercise. The reward was not just calming but a sense of accomplishment in managing stress without harmful eating.

By consciously linking the same trigger (stress) to a healthier routine, Mark rewired his habit loop. Over weeks, his brain started craving the calm from mindfulness instead of the quick sugar rush. His emotional trigger was still there, but the habit response was transformed.

Mark's story shows that habits are not destiny; understanding triggers lets us reclaim choice over our responses and craft healthier habit cycles.

## Why Emotions and Triggers Matter Together

To summarize:

**Triggers start habits** by signaling the brain to initiate the learned routine.

**Emotions cement habits** by attaching rewarding feelings that make repetition desirable.

Without emotional reward, even repeated behaviors struggle to become habits.

Without clear triggers, habits don't reliably initiate.

Together, they form the backbone of the habit loop that powers much of our daily behavior.

## Practical Steps to Harness Emotions and Triggers

To master your habits, consider these strategies:

**Identify your triggers.** Keep a journal for a few days to note when habits kick in and what cue may be causing it.

**Use healthy triggers.** Place reminders or visual cues in your environment to prompt desired routines (like a water bottle to trigger hydration).

**Design positive emotional rewards.** Insert small pleasures or celebrations into your habit routines to generate dopamine releases.

**Change the routine when stuck.** Keep the same trigger and reward but replace the routine with a better option.

**Pause and reflect on emotional states.** Catch emotional triggers before they drive you into automatic, unwanted habits.

## You Are the Architect of Your Habits

The wiring of habits in the brain shows us something profound: habits are mighty but not immutable. By understanding how your brain responds to triggers and rewards and how emotions bind these together, you gain the ultimate power to rewrite your behavioral patterns.

Your triggers and emotions are like notes and rhythms in a personal symphony—learn to conduct them with intention, and you can create music that lifts your life instead of noise that holds you back. Every habit begins in the brain with a cue and a feeling. But it ends with your awareness and choice.

## Neuroplasticity: Your Brain's Capacity to Rewire

Neuroplasticity is the biological basis for change in habits. It is the brain's dynamic ability to reorganize neural pathways by forming new connections and pruning away unused ones, influenced by experience, learning, and practice. This adaptability explains how behaviors that once took tremendous effort become automatic, and how entrenched habits can eventually be modified or replaced.

Imagine walking through a dense forest. The first time you forge a path, it's slow and exhausting. With each walk, the path becomes clearer, wider, and easier. This is neuroplasticity at work—the brain's circuits simplify and reinforce a repeated behavior. But if you divert to a different trail and neglect the old one, that original path becomes overgrown and forgotten.

No matter your age or previous habits, neuroplasticity gives you the hope and power to build new trails in your brain—the building blocks of new habits.

## The Two Phases: Habit Formation and Habit Execution

When we talk about habits, it's essential to distinguish between two closely related but fundamentally different phases:

**Habit Formation:** This is the learning phase. It is the period when a behavior transitions from conscious effort to automaticity. The prefrontal cortex—the brain's center for decision-making and self-control—is heavily involved here, working to remember cues, repeat routines, and anticipate rewards. Habit formation demands attention, motivation, and patience.

**Habit Execution:** Once a habit is formed, its execution becomes a streamlined, mostly unconscious process. This stage engages the basal ganglia, the brain region specializing in routine, automatic actions. Habit execution means performing the behavior easily and often without bringing it to conscious thought, saving mental energy.

## Neuroplasticity in Habit Formation

During habit formation, your brain is busy creating new neural circuits. At first, it feels awkward or requires willpower because your brain balances the novelty of the new behavior with existing patterns.

Neuroplasticity shows that repetition over time strengthens the neural pathways that encode the new habit loop. The more you practice the cue-routine-reward sequence, the more your brain transforms the behavior into a well-worn highway.

Dopamine, the brain's reward chemical, plays a crucial role by reinforcing the positive feelings associated with the rewards, motivating the brain to repeat the behavior.

## Sophia's Path to Mindful Eating

Sophia struggled with emotional eating. Her formation phase began when she consciously decided to change—recognizing the cues of stress that triggered unhealthy snacking. She replaced her eating routine with deep breathing and journaling before meals to pause and assess emotions.

At first, the habit was fragile and effortful. But with consistent repetition, Sophia's brain started to rewire. The cues still triggered her, but her routine changed, shifting neural pathways from automatic snacking to mindful actions. Neuroplasticity was reshaping her behaviors daily.

What helped Sophia sustain change was recognizing the difference between how hard habit formation felt and how powerful habit execution would become once breezed through.

## The Science of Habit Execution

Habit execution is the brain performing well-established routines with autonomy and minimal conscious interference. When habits become part of the basal ganglia's domain, execution feels effortless and reliable. The behavior springs out as soon as the cue occurs, providing the reward that seals the loop.

But here is the subtlety: habit execution itself can vary in complexity. Researchers distinguish between:

> **Instigation (or initiation) habits:** The automatic impulse to start a behavior when triggered.

> **Execution habits:** The smooth and automatic performance of the steps that complete the behavior.

For example, you might habitually instigate running once your running shoes are visible at the door (instigation), but the execution—the detailed sequence of lacing up, stretching, running—may still require some conscious adjustment or motivation.

This distinction highlights why some people find beginning actions easy but struggle with consistent execution or perseverance.

## Michael's Exercise Struggle

Michael was motivated to exercise but couldn't stay consistent. His instigation habit was strong—seeing his gym clothes pushed him to start workouts—but his execution habit was weak. Sometimes, during workouts, he flagged, skipped parts, or quit early.

By focusing on building execution habits, Michael introduced simple routines in his sessions, such as starting with five minutes of stretching and slowly increasing workout complexity. Over time, these micro-habits helped his execution become automatic, boosting overall consistency.

Michael's experience shows that habit change requires attention not only to starting behaviors but also to how they're carried out and maintained.

## Rewiring Old Habits Using Neuroplasticity

Changing a habit means disrupting existing neural circuits and making new, healthier pathways stronger.

> **Breaking old pathways:** Reduce exposure to cues or change emotions linked to the habit to weaken automatic responses.

**Building new circuits:** Consistently pair old cues with new routines and satisfying rewards.

**Repetition with intention:** Neuroplasticity is slow; repeated practice is essential.

**Emotional engagement:** Dopamine release makes new habits "stick." Make rewards meaningful.

By understanding which phase you're in—formation or execution—you can tailor strategies and be patient with the process.

## Lisa's Journey Off Social Media

Lisa realized she spent too much time scrolling through social media, a habit that distracted and drained her. She noticed her habit loop: boredom or anxiety (cue), checking phone (routine), temporary distraction and social connection (reward).

Changing this wasn't simple. In the formation phase, Lisa resisted the urge and replaced her routine with reading books or talking to friends. These efforts felt tiring because her brain still craved the old reward.

After weeks of repetition, her brain started to rewire. Phone checking became less automatic—it no longer immediately relieved boredom. Lisa's execution habit for managing free time gradually transformed, creating new neural pathways aligned with her goals.

This process reveals the profound interplay of neuroplasticity and habit phases in real life.

## Practical Tips: Applying Neuroplasticity Across Habit Phases

**For habit formation:** Focus on small, manageable steps. Use conscious effort to build new pathways.

**For habit execution:** Simplify routines to strengthen automatic pathways and reduce decision fatigue.

**Use environmental design:** Place cues that support new habits and reduce old cue exposure.

**Embrace failure:** Neuroplasticity means trying again; setbacks don't erase progress.

**Celebrate progress:** Positive emotions energize dopamine release, enhancing rewiring.

## Habits Are Paths You Can Reshape

Your brain's wonderful capacity for neuroplasticity means that no habit is set in stone. Understanding that habit formation and habit execution are distinct phases supported by different brain systems allows for wiser strategies tailored to your unique journey.

Whether you are starting fresh or deepening your routines, your brain can create and maintain habits that serve your best self—and neuroplasticity is your lifelong ally, crafting your habits one repeated choice at a time.

# Chapter Three

## Identifying and Eliminating Tiny Bad Habits

**Common Hidden Bad Habits to Watch For**

Tiny bad habits often fly under the radar of our daily awareness. They might seem insignificant, harmless even, but over time, they accumulate and shape our reality in ways we don't immediately notice. These habits can sneak into our routines, quietly siphoning energy and productivity or impacting our relationships and self-esteem.

This chapter shines a light on some of the most common hidden bad habits, helping you to recognize them firsthand. Awareness is the first crucial step in transforming them into positive habits.

## The Sneaky Saboteurs: Tiny Bad Habits Around Us

**Mindless scrolling on phones**: Most of us reach for our phones unconsciously, especially during breaks or first thing in the morning. What starts as a quick check often turns into a binge of social media or news that steals precious time and focus.

**Procrastinating on small tasks**: Delaying small chores or responsibilities may seem trivial, but procrastination builds stress and backlog. It chips away at self-discipline and creates a habit where putting things off becomes second nature.

**Interrupting others**: In conversations, interrupting might feel like you're being engaged and interested, but it actually sends a message of disrespect. It also stifles meaningful dialogue and connection.

**Excessive multitasking**: Trying to juggle multiple things at once can reduce productivity and increase mistakes. It may seem efficient but actually fragments concentration and leads to burnout.

**Negative self-talk**: Internal dialogues that criticize, doubt, or diminish can slowly erode confidence.

Hidden from others, these harmful thoughts sabotage motivation and create mental blocks.

**Skipping breaks or meals**: Ignoring the body's signals for rest or nourishment to power through work can drain energy and impair health. This habit disguises itself as productivity but undermines long-term effectiveness.

**Overcommitting and saying yes too often**: Agreeing to every request without setting boundaries causes overwhelm and resentment. This bad habit drains time and attention from personal goals or self-care.

### Emma's Battle with Tiny Time Thieves

Emma, a 34-year-old marketing executive, thought she was "too busy" to notice anything wrong with how she spent her day. Yet, she felt exhausted, unaccomplished, and disconnected from her passions. Emma's story is a common journey many can relate to.

One day, Emma took a simple step that turned her life around. She decided to track what she did each hour for a week. The results shocked her. She realized she was spending more than two hours a day scrolling on her phone, mostly on social media and random videos. She also caught herself frequently jumping between emails, calls, and reports without finishing any task thoroughly.

Her negative self-talk was screaming too—phrases like "I'm not good enough," "I'm always behind" echoed in her mind. These tiny habits combined to create a cycle of stress and dissatisfaction.

Emma began to tackle these hidden bad habits slowly but deliberately. She set strict phone-free time blocks, practiced mindful breathing before responding to emails, and challenged negative thoughts by writing down positive affirmations daily.

Over the following months, Emma noticed her energy rising, her focus sharpening, and her self-confidence growing. She realized these once-small habits had been quietly holding her back from living fully.

Emma's story reminds us that no matter how subtle, these habits influence the big picture and that recognizing and addressing them is an act of self-care.

## How to Spot Your Hidden Bad Habits

To identify your tiny hidden bad habits, consider:

> Where do you lose track of time daily?

> What automatic behaviors trigger stress or regret?

> Which thoughts repeat in your mind that discourage or criticize you?

> Are there small health or lifestyle routines you neglect regularly?

> When do you feel worst during your day and what habits precede that?

Writing down answers to these questions can start revealing patterns you hadn't noticed. Honest reflection creates a foundation to create targeted change.

## Example of Hidden Bad Habits in Everyday Life

Take the story of Mark, a father who felt constantly exhausted and disconnected from his family despite working long hours.

Mark realized his habit of checking work emails late at night — just "for a minute" — was a hidden bad habit eating into his family time and rest. When he consciously set boundaries, such as turning off email notifications after 8pm, he reclaimed evenings to engage with his kids fully. This tiny shift greatly improved his mood and family dynamics.

### Common Hidden Bad Habits Checklist

Excessive screen time outside work or study

Chronic procrastination on small tasks

Interrupting or talking over others in conversations

Constant multitasking reducing quality focus

Persistent negative self-talk or self-criticism

Skipping meals or breaks to "save time"

Saying yes to too many obligations without limits

Ignoring physical exercise or self-care routines

Holding grudges or dwelling on small irritations

Relying on caffeine or sugar excessively as energy boosts

Each habit may seem minor but identifying them is key before trying to change.

Recognizing and eliminating hidden bad habits is the groundwork for sustainable personal improvement. This chapter invites reflection on these subtle behaviors and encourages gentle, consistent steps toward healthier patterns. Small changes, repeated daily, lead to transformational growth.

## Understanding Why Bad Habits Persist

Bad habits endure because they fulfill deep psychological and neurological functions that become automatic over time. At the core, habits are formed through a three-step loop in the brain: a cue triggers a behavior, which leads to a reward, reinforcing the behavior's repetition. Even when habits are detrimental, the immediate reward—such as relief from stress, a momentary escape, or a small dopamine rush—keeps the cycle intact. This reward system creates strong neural pathways that make bad habits automatic, requiring less conscious effort to perform and harder to break.

Another reason bad habits persist is the brain's natural bias for short-term gratification over long-term benefits. Even when the negative consequences are understood logically, the brain often prioritizes immediate pleasure. For example, someone might know that procrastinating causes stress, but the short-term comfort of avoiding a difficult task feels more compelling.

Cognitive distortions reinforce persistence too. Rationalizing bad habits ("I'll just do it once," or "I work better under pressure") serve as excuses that justify continued behavior without accountability.

This mental resistance to change creates internal conflicts that keep bad habits alive.

Moreover, environmental and social cues play a critical role. Surroundings, routines, and even people can trigger habits without conscious awareness. A person trying to eat healthily might struggle if their environment is full of junk food or if their social circle encourages unhealthy eating. These external reinforcers make habit change a layered challenge that requires more than willpower.

## The Cost of Bad Habits on Productivity

The impact of bad habits on productivity is profound and often underestimated. Productivity involves not just working hard but working smart and efficiently. Bad habits undermine this by wasting critical resources—time, energy, focus, and motivation.

**Time Drain:** One of the biggest killers of productivity is constant distractions, like frequently checking emails or social media. Every interruption breaks concentration and can cost up to 20-25 minutes of refocusing time when returning to the original task. For example, a worker who checks their phone every 10 minutes could lose several hours of productive time daily.

**Reduced Focus:** Multitasking is a common bad habit that significantly reduces productivity. Although it feels like getting more done, multitasking fragments attention and increases errors. The brain is not wired to perform well on multiple demanding tasks simultaneously, leading to lower quality outcomes and slower completion times.

**Procrastination:** Delaying difficult or unpleasant tasks leads to a cycle of stress and rushing. Procrastinators often tackle less important work to avoid challenges, which crowds out time for high-priority tasks. This habit worsens workload and diminishes the sense of accomplishment.

**Energy Drain:** Skipping breaks or meals to "save time" can backfire by lowering physical and mental energy. Fatigue impairs cognitive function, decision-making, and creativity—all essential for productive work. Sustainable productivity requires regular rest and nourishment.

**Negative Self-Talk:** Persistently doubting oneself or engaging in harsh self-criticism erosion motivation and resilience. This internal sabotage creates hesitance to tackle challenges or pursue ambitious goals, limiting potential achievements.

**Overcommitment:** Saying yes to everything because of poor boundaries leads to overwhelm and burnout. When attention is spread too thin across too many tasks or projects, none get the focused effort they need for success.

**Impact on Teamwork:** Bad habits like interrupting, disorganization, or poor communication also disrupt team productivity. They create friction and inefficiencies, reducing collective output and morale.

## Lisa's Struggle with Unseen Habits

Lisa, a driven entrepreneur, believed that working harder and longer hours was the key to success. Yet, she felt exhausted and unfulfilled. Despite her commitment, progress felt slow, and distractions robbed her of focus. She was a master of multitasking but rarely finished tasks on time. The constant email checking and phone notifications fragmented her attention, making deep, creative work impossible.

One evening, burned out and frustrated, Lisa confided in a mentor. The mentor recommended a simple habit-tracking exercise: for a week, Lisa logged every activity and her thoughts about it. This vulnerable act revealed how frequently she succumbed to distractions and how often negative thoughts told her she wasn't doing enough, fostering a sense of inadequacy.

With this new awareness, Lisa began small but deliberate changes. She blocked off focused work times with her phone and email turned off. She made a conscious effort to tackle her hardest tasks first thing in the morning when energy and focus were highest. She practiced kindness in her self-talk, replacing "I'll never get this done" with "I'm making progress every day."

Over months, Lisa's productivity skyrocketed—not because she worked more, but because she worked smarter and healed her relationship with work and herself. Her story exemplifies that hidden habits, though tiny, have huge effects—and recognizing them is the first step toward lasting transformation.

## Common Bad Habits That Hurt Productivity

**Constantly checking emails and notifications:** Interruptions rob focus and waste time with frequent context switching.

**Multitasking:** Dividing attention reduces efficiency and quality of work.

**Procrastinating difficult tasks:** Avoidance leads to backlog, stress, and lower accomplishment.

**Negative self-talk:** Internal discouragement limits confidence and motivation.

**Skipping breaks and meals:** Lack of rest and nourishment drains energy and cognitive function.

**Overcommitting:** Poor boundaries create overwhelm and scatter attention.

**Surfing the web aimlessly:** Unsanctioned web browsing causes significant time loss.

**Doing easy tasks first:** Prioritizing less challenging tasks leaves important work unfinished.

**Rationalizing excuses:** Justifying bad habits prevents owning the need for change.

## Why Awareness Leads to Power

The hidden nature of these bad habits means they often operate outside conscious control. Taking time to observe daily routines, thoughts, and behaviors uncovers crucial insights. Without awareness, efforts to improve productivity hit invisible walls. Tracking habits with honesty creates clarity and identifies specific targets for change.

Instead of fighting vague "bad habits," knowing exactly which ones drain time and energy enables focused interventions—like scheduling distraction-free work blocks, practicing time blocking, or planning manageable daily goals. These intentional changes overhaul productivity and well-being.

Lisa's story proves that when bad habits are spotlighted, they lose their power. Transformation is possible by replacing detrimental routines with sustainable, positive habits. The cost of ignoring these habits is wasted potential; the reward of addressing them is reclaiming control and fulfillment.

## Techniques to Interrupt Bad Habit Loops

Breaking free from bad habits requires understanding the fundamental "habit loop" — a cycle consisting of a cue (trigger), a routine (behavior), and a reward (the benefit you get). This loop creates a neurological pattern in your brain, making the habit automatic and difficult to break. To interrupt this cycle, specific techniques can be employed:

**Identify the Habit Loop:** Start by becoming fully aware of the cue that triggers the habit, the routine you go through, and the reward you seek. Keep a journal to track when and where the habit arises, your feelings at that moment, and what you gain from it. This awareness is crucial to disrupting the cycle.

**Change the Cue:** Altering or avoiding environmental triggers can prevent automatic behavior. For instance, if snacking late at night is triggered by watching TV, removing snacks from the living room or changing your evening routine can help. Avoiding social or physical contexts that encourage the habit is effective, like steering clear of certain places or people associated with it.

**Replace the Routine:** Instead of just trying to stop the behavior, substitute it with a healthier alternative that satisfies the same need or craving. If stress causes you to grab junk food, replace it with a brief walk or deep breathing exercises. This maintains the reward mechanism while shifting the routine toward a positive habit.

**Use Habit Reversal Training:** This involves increasing awareness of the habit's early signs and intentionally performing a competing behavior incompatible with the bad habit. For example, someone who picks nails might clench fists instead when feeling the urge.

**Employ Cognitive Restructuring:** Challenge negative thoughts that justify or perpetuate the habit. Replace them with realistic and positive thinking to weaken mental resistance to change.

**Plan Ahead:** Anticipate moments when the habit tends to appear and prepare strategies to manage these triggers. For a habit like procrastination, breaking tasks into tiny steps and scheduling focused time blocks can prevent old patterns.

**Practice Mindfulness:** Increasing present-moment awareness helps catch the habit before it happens, offering a chance to consciously choose a different action.

**Habit Stacking:** Link a new habit to an existing one. For instance, after brushing your teeth, spend two minutes stretching. This makes forming positive habits easier and helps crowd out destructive ones.

# Replacing Destructive Behaviors with Awareness

Awareness is the foundation for replacing destructive behaviors with constructive ones. It involves realizing not just the habit itself, but the underlying emotions, thoughts, and needs driving it.

**Recognize Emotional Triggers:** Many habits arise as coping mechanisms for emotions like stress, boredom, or loneliness. Becoming attuned to these feelings helps uncouple the automatic response. Instead of mindlessly scrolling social media when stressed, pause and identify the emotion before choosing a healthier alternative.

**Observe Your Thoughts:** Reflect on internal dialogues that prompt or justify the behavior. Negative self-talk can keep you locked in cycles of failure or procrastination. Awareness allows deliberate interruption of such thoughts, replacing them with encouraging and optimistic patterns.

**Keep a Habit Diary:** Recording not only the habit but also the context—time, place, mood—sharpens insight into patterns. This information guides the creation of tailored replacement strategies.

**Create Replacement Rituals:** Develop simple, enjoyable alternatives that meet the same reward need. For example, if smoking provides a sense of relaxation, replace it with sipping herbal tea or doing gentle stretches.

**Celebrate Small Wins:** Positive reinforcement helps strengthen new habits. Recognize every step forward as progress, bolstering motivation and resilience.

## How Sarah Broke Free from Her Social Media Trap

Sarah, a young professional, found herself trapped in the endless scroll of social media every day after work. She felt frustrated about the hours lost and the way it drained her energy but struggled to stop. She realized her habit was triggered by the cue of sitting down on the couch after a long day—a moment she associated with unwinding.

To interrupt her habit loop, Sarah first tracked her behavior, noting how often she opened apps and what feelings prompted it. The reward was clear: distraction from work stress and a fleeting sense of connection. Aware now, Sarah began changing cues by leaving her phone in another room when she got home. She replaced the routine of scrolling with a new ritual: making a cup of tea and reading a chapter of her favorite book.

Sarah also used mindfulness, catching herself reaching for the phone and consciously deciding to breathe deeply instead. She challenged her thoughts like "I need to relax by scrolling" and replaced them with "I can relax in healthier ways that really refresh me."

It wasn't easy, and sometimes she slipped. But over weeks, her new habits strengthened, her anxiety decreased, and she felt more present in her life. Sarah's story shows that with awareness and strategic replacement, destructive habits are not permanent chains but changeable patterns.

Interrupting bad habit loops involves conscious disruption of the cue-routine-reward cycle. Techniques like identifying habit components, changing triggers, substituting routines, and employing cognitive strategies reshape automatic behavior. Awareness deepens understanding of the emotional and mental drivers behind habits, paving the way for healthier replacements. Stories like

**Sarah's illuminate that change, though challenging, is achievable with patience, self-compassion, and consistent effort.**

# Chapter Four

## Cultivating Tiny Good Habits to Create Change

### Essential Habits for Productivity Enhancement

Productivity is not the result of one grand action but the sum of many small, positive habits practiced consistently over time. Cultivating tiny good habits builds momentum, rewires the brain for focus, and accelerates meaningful progress. Below are essential habits that enhance productivity when incorporated deliberately in daily life.

### Prioritize the Most Important Tasks (MITs)

One of the most impactful habits is identifying and starting your day with the Most Important Tasks (MITs). These are the top 1-3 high-value tasks that drive significant results. Tackling MITs first, when energy and focus are highest, creates a cascade of productivity for the rest of the day. This habit prevents the trap of spending most time on low-value or urgent but unimportant activities.

## Cultivate Deep Work

Deep work means dedicating uninterrupted blocks of time to single focused tasks without distractions. This habit maximizes cognitive performance, enabling you to get into a state of flow where quality and quantity of output rise. Scheduling focused 60-90 minute sessions, turning off notifications, and closing unrelated tabs are effective ways to practice deep work.

## Maintain a Distraction List

Interruptions often derail productivity. Keeping a 'distraction list' by your workspace allows you to quickly jot down distracting thoughts or tasks that pop into your head without acting on them immediately. This preserves focus while ensuring nothing important is forgotten, reducing cognitive overload.

## Use the Eisenhower Matrix

Effectively managing priorities involves distinguishing between urgent and important tasks. The Eisenhower Matrix categorizes tasks into four quadrants: urgent and important, important but not urgent, urgent but not important, and neither. Developing the habit of regularly plotting tasks in this matrix guides time and effort toward what truly matters and prevents reactive task management.

## Break Tasks into Smaller Steps

Large tasks can seem daunting and trigger procrastination. Breaking tasks into smaller, manageable steps creates a clear roadmap and reduces overwhelm. Each small step becomes a tiny win, maintaining motivation and forward momentum.

## Take Regular Breaks

Working non-stop drains mental and physical energy. Incorporating breaks, such as the Pomodoro Technique's 25 minutes of work followed by 5-minute breaks, refreshes the brain and prevents burnout. Structured breaks improve long-term focus and stamina.

## Keep a Consistent Morning Routine

Starting the day with intentional habits—hydrating, light exercise, meditation, or journaling—sets a positive tone and builds mental readiness. A consistent morning routine strengthens discipline and signals the brain to shift into productive mode.

## Practice Saying No

Highly productive people protect their time fiercely. Learning to say no to non-essential meetings, tasks, or distractions maintains boundaries and reserves energy for high-impact activities. This habit combats overcommitment and enhances focus.

## Organize Workspace and Digital Environment

A tidy physical and digital workspace reduces stress and decision fatigue. Organizing files, decluttering desks, and streamlining digital tools creates an environment conducive to efficiency and creativity.

## James's Transformation Through Tiny Habits

James, a freelance graphic designer, always struggled with inconsistent productivity. His creative bursts were followed by days of feeling overwhelmed and procrastinating on deadlines. Feeling stuck, James decided to focus on cultivating small good habits rather than making sweeping changes.

He began by identifying his MITs every morning, writing them on a sticky note on his desk. He committed to working for 25 minutes uninterrupted and then taking a 5-minute break, gradually increasing the focus time. James also created a distraction list, capturing distracting ideas so he could defer dealing with them.

By reorganizing his workspace, removing clutter and setting clear work and rest boundaries, James noticed a remarkable change. His days became more structured, deadlines were met with ease, and stress levels dropped. The momentum from these tiny habits helped him build confidence, leading to bigger improvements, such as a consistent morning routine and mastering deep work sessions.

James's experience exemplifies how small, consistent habits can transform productivity not overnight but steadily—with patience and self-kindness.

The essence of productivity enhancement lies in cultivating tiny, essential habits that align with long-term goals. By focusing on prioritization, focused effort, managing distractions, structuring work, and protecting energy, anyone can progressively increase their effectiveness. The heart of habit change is recognizing that success is built one small step at a time, not by leaps. Approach each day with intention, practice these foundational habits, and watch your productivity blossom.

## Building Habits Around Your Daily Routine

Habits thrive best when seamlessly integrated into the rhythm of your daily life. Building habits around your daily routine means weaving them into existing activities and cues rather than trying to overhaul your entire day at once. This approach leverages natural momentum and reduces resistance, making habit formation sustainable.

A powerful technique is "habit stacking," where you attach a new habit to an established one. For example, after brushing your teeth in the morning, you might immediately do five minutes of stretching or write a daily intention journal entry. The cue (teeth brushing) naturally triggers the new habit, automating the behavior over time.

Creating a predictable daily schedule further supports habits. Waking up and going to bed at consistent times signals your body and mind to prepare for certain actions, like exercising or reading.

Adding small habits at specific times—drinking water right after waking, taking a brief walk after lunch, or planning the next day before bed—anchors behaviors to times when you're most receptive.

Breaking the day into ritualized segments, such as morning routines, work sprints, and evening wind-downs, helps to situate habits into manageable chunks. This helps reduce decision fatigue by creating clear mental pathways: the brain knows what to expect at each phase of your day.

Environmental cues also play a role in embedding daily habits. For instance, keeping workout clothes visible promotes exercise, while a tidy desk primes focused work sessions. Aligning your environment with your routines supports habit automation by subtly steering behavior.

## How Small Wins Lead to Big Results

Small wins are the building blocks of lasting change. They provide tangible evidence of progress, boost motivation, and build momentum. Achieving even minor goals releases dopamine, the brain's "feel-good" chemical, reinforcing behaviors and encouraging repetition.

Instead of aiming for massive overnight transformations, focusing on achievable, incremental progress cultivates consistency. Each small win, whether completing a 10-minute workout, successfully avoiding distractions for one Pomodoro session, or drinking an extra glass of water, compounds over time into significant results.

Small wins foster psychological resilience. When you celebrate progress—even small—it counteracts feelings of discouragement and builds confidence. This is particularly important when facing setbacks, as recognizing wins helps maintain an upward trajectory.

This concept can be seen in weight loss, learning new skills, or productivity improvements. Someone trying to get fit doesn't need to run 5 miles on day one; instead, walking around the block consistently is a small win leading to bigger gains. A writer's daily habit of 200 words builds effortlessly into a finished book over months.

## Maria's Journey of Tiny Changes

Maria, a busy mother and office worker, struggled to find time for personal goals amid the chaos of daily responsibilities. She felt overwhelmed by the idea of massive lifestyle changes. A friend suggested starting with tiny habits anchored to daily routines.

Maria began by drinking a glass of water immediately after brushing her teeth each morning—a simple step but one she could easily maintain. Gradually, she added a two-minute morning stretch routine right after. These small successes lifted her spirits and gave her a sense of accomplishment early in each day.

She tracked progress in a journal, celebrating every completed habit stack. Inspired by small wins, Maria started setting five-minute timed focus sessions during work and took short walks during breaks. Over weeks, these manageable habits improved her energy, focus, and mood.

Maria's story reveals that gentle, incremental steps woven into daily life disrupt overwhelm and create real transformation. Small wins build a foundation of sustainable change, turning intention into action and dreams into reality.

## Practical Tips for Building Habits Into Your Routine

Identify natural daily cues to anchor new habits.

Start with tiny versions of habits to ensure success.

Use habit stacking to piggyback new behaviors onto existing ones.

Maintain consistency by linking habits to the same time or place.

Adjust routines as needed but keep foundational habits intact.

Reward yourself for small wins to strengthen habit loops.

Reflect weekly on progress to reinforce motivation.

## Habit Stacking: Linking New Habits to Old Ones

Habit stacking is a powerful technique for building new habits effortlessly by anchoring them to already established behaviors in your daily routine. This method leverages the natural momentum and cues of existing habits to create seamless opportunities to adopt new, positive behaviors.

The basic formula for habit stacking is simple:
**After (or before) I do [current habit], I will do [new habit].**

For example, if you already make a morning cup of coffee every day, you might stack a new habit like this:
"After I pour my morning cup of coffee, I will meditate for one minute."

Or in the evening, after finishing dinner, you might stack:
"After I put my dishes in the dishwasher, I will wipe down the kitchen counter."

This approach uses the cue from your existing habit—pouring coffee, finishing dinner—to naturally trigger the new behavior, making it easier for your brain to adopt the new pattern without needing extra motivation or willpower.

Habit stacking can grow into chains of habits, where one habit leads into another, creating a fluid routine. For instance:

> After I brush my teeth, I will floss.

> After I floss, I will wash my face.

> After I wash my face, I will read one page of a book.

Breaking down behaviors into these small, linked actions lowers resistance to change and builds consistency. The familiarity of the original habit cue creates certainty, which is comforting to your brain.

Habit stacking also helps in expanding routines. Say you already have a morning routine of waking up, making your bed, and taking a shower. To build reading into your day, you could stack placing a book on your pillow after making your bed, so when you go to sleep, the book is ready and waiting.

## Tracking Your Progress for Motivation

Tracking progress is crucial for maintaining motivation and reinforcing new habits. When you can see your hard work accumulating over days, weeks, and months, it provides tangible proof of change, encouraging persistence.

Several methods for habit tracking can help:

**Habit Journals**: Writing daily whether you completed the habit or not helps bring awareness and accountability. It's also a place to reflect on obstacles and feelings related to the habit.

**Habit Trackers and Apps**: Visual trackers in apps or on paper calendars use checkmarks or symbols for each day the habit is completed. Seeing a long chain of successful days can create "chain momentum," motivating you to avoid breaking the streak.

**Reward Systems**: Linking progress to small rewards can boost motivation. For instance, if you complete a habit for a week straight, treat yourself to a favorite activity or item.

Tracking also enables problem-solving. If you notice regular missed days, you can review and adjust the habit, routine, or triggers to improve success.

## Tom's Habit Stacking and Tracking Journey

Tom, a software developer, struggled with maintaining a consistent exercise routine. Motivation would flare up briefly but fade without structure. A friend introduced him to habit stacking and tracking.

Tom identified his existing morning habit: brewing his coffee. He added a small new habit: doing five push-ups right after pouring coffee. Using the formula, "After I pour coffee, I will do five push-ups," he anchored the new behavior to the strong existing cue.

At first, it was just five push-ups, but soon, it became enjoyable and motivating. Tom expanded the stack to include stretching and a short walk after his push-ups. It became a natural part of his morning.

He started tracking progress on a simple calendar, marking every day he completed his exercise stack. The visible chain grew longer, and he didn't want to break the streak. He rewarded every 10 consecutive days with a small gift to himself.

A couple of months later, Tom's tiny stacks transformed his fitness and energy. He credits habit stacking and tracking for making change feel achievable rather than overwhelming.

Habit stacking connects new behaviors to existing ones, turning isolated efforts into consistent routines through logical and reliable cues. This technique reduces friction in adopting new habits by piggybacking on the familiar, making change simpler and more sustainable.

Tracking your progress provides motivation by making abstract effort concrete. Whether through journals, apps, or calendars, visible evidence of habit completion fuels consistency and helps navigate obstacles with insight.

Tom's story illustrates how linking habits and tracking progress creates momentum that turns small daily actions into lasting transformation, showing anyone can build positive change with a kind, structured approach.

# Chapter Five

## The Process of Changing Habits Effectively

The 1% Improvement Principle and Its Power

Changing habits effectively is less about giant leaps and more about consistent, small improvements. This principle of making just 1% progress daily can unlock remarkable transformations over time. The 1% improvement principle emphasizes that tiny, incremental gains compound, leading to exponential growth in productivity, health, or personal development. This approach dismantles the myth that change requires overwhelming effort and instead focuses on steady, achievable progress.

### Understanding the 1% Improvement Principle

The essence of the 1% improvement principle lies in marginal gains—the concept that small enhancements in various areas add up to a big overall improvement. For instance, improving by just 1% each day doesn't seem impactful at first glance, but mathematically, it leads to doubling your effectiveness in about 70 days. This is because daily improvements multiply rather than add, creating a powerful compounding effect.

This principle is backed by psychological research on habit formation and behavior change. Habits form gradually through repetition and reinforcement in consistent contexts, often taking around 66 days on average for the behavior to become automatic. The 1% rule encourages patience with the process, supporting repeated small actions until they become part of your natural routine.

By focusing on incremental progress rather than perfection, the principle also reduces overwhelm and combats procrastination. When change feels manageable, motivation is sustained. It shifts the mindset from "I have to overhaul everything at once" to "What is one small step I can take right now?"

## How the 1% Principle Works in Everyday Life

Consider someone wanting to improve fitness. Attempting to run a marathon immediately may feel impossible and deter effort. However, committing to adding one additional minute to a daily walk or doing one extra push-up gradually builds endurance without burnout. Over weeks, these tiny steps build strength, confidence, and a habit of exercise.

Similarly, for productivity, starting with setting one tiny goal each day, such as organizing a single document or spending five focused minutes on a project, creates momentum. Each day's small win fuels motivation for the next, eventually leading to significant cumulative progress.

## Anna's Journey of 1% Daily Growth

Anna, a writer struggling with self-doubt and inconsistency, felt stuck in a cycle of starting and abandoning projects. She was overwhelmed by the expectation that successful writing required long hours or massive output overnight.

A mentor introduced her to the 1% improvement principle and suggested she commit to writing just 50 words a day—an achievable and non-intimidating goal. Initially, this felt minor, but Anna noticed the psychological change. Writing daily built a positive identity around being "a consistent writer" rather than "someone who struggles to write."

Over time, the 50 words naturally expanded to 100, then 200 and beyond. The compound effect transformed Anna's productivity and confidence. More importantly, the practice brought joy back to her work, with pressure replaced by progress.

Anna's story exemplifies that monumental change starts with microscopic steps, each reinforcing the belief that improvement is possible and sustainable.

## Implementing the 1% Improvement Principle

**Set small, specific goals:** Identify tiny steps aligned with your bigger objectives. Make them so achievable that saying "no" is unlikely.

**Focus on consistency:** Prioritize showing up daily rather than performance perfection. Frequent repetition solidifies habits.

**Measure progress:** Track small wins to generate motivation and evidence of improvement. Visual trackers can boost commitment.

**Be patient:** Understand habit formation takes time—usually several weeks to months depending on the behavior.

**Adjust and optimize:** Regularly reflect and refine your approach but avoid drastic changes that disrupt momentum.

**Celebrate wins:** Even minor progress deserves acknowledgment, reinforcing positive feelings about growth.

## Psychological Insights Behind the Power of 1%

Behavioral science shows that habits operate via cue-routine-reward loops. Each small improvement tweaks this loop slightly, reinforcing a new neural pathway. Because habits become automatic with repetition, the 1% principle taps into these gradual neurological changes.

Additionally, focusing on small wins maintains dopamine release, the brain's reward chemistry, fostering desire and motivation to continue. It reduces decision fatigue and breaks cycles of inertia linked to overwhelming goals.

The 1% improvement principle is a potent, scientifically backed framework for effective habit change. It champions small daily progressions that harness the brain's habit formation mechanisms and the power of compounding growth. Through patient, manageable steps, anyone can create sustainable change without feeling overwhelmed. Heartfelt stories like Anna's illuminate the transformative potential of embracing this humble but mighty principle.

Using this approach, changing habits becomes not a daunting challenge but an achievable journey of continuous growth.

## Using Tiny Goals for Sustainable Growth

Sustainable growth in habits and personal improvement is best achieved through tiny, manageable goals. These small goals avoid overwhelming the individual, creating a sense of progress that is both tangible and motivating. Tiny goals serve as stepping stones for larger aspirations by making change approachable and maintainable over the long term.

The core idea behind tiny goals is to break down large ambitions into the smallest actionable step possible. For instance, rather than "write a chapter," start with "write one sentence." Over time, the accumulation of these incremental efforts creates momentum and a snowball effect of achievement.

Tiny goals reduce resistance by minimizing the effort required to start. The brain naturally favors immediate rewards and avoids daunting challenges, so the simplicity of tiny goals lowers the barrier to entry. This reduces procrastination and builds consistency—two key factors in sustainable growth.

Tiny goals align well with the psychology of habit formation. Research suggests habits form through repeated actions in consistent contexts. Tiny goals increase the likelihood of repetition by being less disruptive and easier to integrate into daily life.

## How Tiny Goals Foster Sustainable Growth

**Builds consistency:** Regular small successes reinforce positive behavior and habit loops.

**Encourages momentum:** Achieving a tiny goal creates motivation to continue and expand efforts.

**Reduces overwhelm:** Breaking tasks into small pieces makes goals feel manageable.

**Increases self-efficacy:** Each completed action builds confidence and belief in ability.

**Supports long-term change:** Tiny goals create durable patterns rather than temporary bursts of effort.

## David's Journey from Overwhelm to Progress

David, an aspiring entrepreneur, dreamed of launching his online business but was paralyzed by the enormity of the effort required. The thought of designing a website, creating marketing content, and managing finances felt impossible all at once. Procrastination and self-doubt dominated his days.

A mentor encouraged David to adopt tiny goals. His first goal was to spend just five minutes a day outlining his business idea. Five minutes felt achievable and removed pressure. Eventually, David's five minutes doubled, and he started drafting his website content one paragraph at a time.

This tiny steps approach helped him build self-discipline and quality output without burnout. He celebrated each completed micro goal, gradually replacing overwhelm and procrastination with steady progress and excitement.

David's story underscores how sustainable growth thrives on tiny goals: manageable, consistent, and confidence-building actions that pave the way toward big dreams.

## Overcoming Procrastination Through Micro Habits

Procrastination is often rooted in fear, perfectionism, or feeling overwhelmed. Micro habits—ultra-small behaviors performed consistently—offer a practical antidote by lowering the activation energy required to start a task.

Instead of committing to hours of work all at once, micro habits encourage starting with just one tiny action, such as opening a project file, writing one sentence, or organizing one desktop folder. These minimal efforts bypass inertia and activate momentum.

The key against procrastination is action, however small it may seem. Micro habits seek to remove internal resistance by making starting effortless. Once begun, many people find it easier to keep going—this is sometimes called the "gateway effect," where small initial steps lead to longer engagement naturally.

Additionally, micro habits reduce the need for motivation, which fluctuates daily. By making habits tiny, actions become less dependent on motivation and more automatic, sustained by routine.

## Practical Tips to Use Micro Habits Against Procrastination

**Define the smallest possible step:** Ask, "What's the tiniest action I can start with now?"

**Set timer-based micro sessions:** Work for just 2-5 minutes to initiate flow.

**Remove barriers to action:** Keep needed materials accessible and minimize distractions.

**Pair micro habits with rewards:** Positive reinforcement strengthens habit loops.

**Be kind to yourself:** Avoid judgment and focus on progress, not perfection.

### Elena's Fight Against Procrastination

Elena, a graduate student, often faced daunting writing tasks. She procrastinated by binge-watching shows or scrolling social media, feeling guilty and stuck in a cycle of delay. Traditional "work longer" advice only added pressure.

She discovered micro habits when a counselor suggested she write just one sentence per day on her thesis. At first, one sentence seemed trivial, but it broke the mental block. Writing that small piece led to writing two, then paragraphs. The act of beginning displaced avoidance.

Elena used a timer to write for five minutes daily, celebrating progress instead of perfection. This gentle routine transformed her procrastination into productive flow, reigniting her passion for research.

Her story highlights how micro habits dissolve procrastination by simplifying starting, enabling sustainable productivity.

Tiny goals and micro habits are complementary strategies that foster sustainable growth and overcome procrastination, respectively. By focusing on the smallest actionable steps, they build consistency, momentum, and confidence while minimizing overwhelm and resistance.

David's journey illustrates how tiny goals take the fear out of big dreams, turning them into achievable steps, while Elena's story shows micro habits' power to break procrastination cycles.

Together, these methods offer a gentle yet powerful roadmap for personal change, proving that profound transformation is possible through small, continuous progress.

## The Chain Habit Method Explained

The Chain Habit Method, often referred to as habit chaining or habit stacking, is a powerful approach to developing new habits by linking them sequentially in a chain of daily actions. Instead of trying to form isolated habits in isolation, this method uses the momentum of one behavior to automatically cue the next, creating a domino effect that builds consistency and reduces reliance on willpower.

The concept is simple yet effective: you start by identifying an existing habit or routine already embedded in your daily life. You then append a new desired habit to this existing behavior, using it as a natural trigger. Over time, habits become connected in a chain, where completing one habit signals the brain to perform the next, forming a smooth routine.

For example, a morning habit chain might look like:

Upon waking up, drink a glass of water.

After drinking water, meditate for two minutes.

After meditating, write down three things you're grateful for.

After gratitude journaling, review your top priority task for the day.

Each habit cues the next, building a flow that feels natural and effortless. This method leverages the brain's preference for routine and reduces decision fatigue by turning a series of actions into an automatic sequence.

In practice, you can build longer chains over time, starting with just two or three linked habits and adding as you gain mastery and confidence. The key is keeping the chain manageable and celebrating each completed link, reinforcing the habit loop.

James Clear popularized this idea in his book *Atomic Habits*, emphasizing how layering habits sequentially transforms behavioral change into a domino effect of positive actions. BJ Fogg's Tiny Habits program also promotes similar principles to create simple, scalable changes.

## How to Apply the Chain Habit Method

**List your existing daily habits:** These are things done regularly without fail, such as brushing teeth, making coffee, or checking email.

**Choose a new habit to link:** Start with a small, easily achievable action related to your goals.

**Use the formula:** "After I [existing habit], I will [new habit]."

**Start small:** Keep new habits tiny to prevent overwhelm and boost success chances.

**Build gradually:** Once the linked habit is stable, add another habit to the chain.

**Track progress:** Use habit trackers or calendars to reinforce momentum.

**Celebrate chains:** Recognize completing the full chain to motivate continuation.

## Sam's Habit Chain Transformation

Sam was an overworked professional struggling with health and focus. His mornings lacked structure, and despite good intentions, he couldn't sustain new healthy habits. Feeling overwhelmed by "too much to do," he started with a simple habit chain.

He anchored his first new habit to an existing one: after brushing his teeth, he placed a bottle of water nearby and drank a glass. Next, after drinking, he did one minute of deep breathing to reduce stress. After breathing, he journaled one positive thought.

Though tiny, this chain brought a calming, intentional start to his day, improving mood and focus. Gradually, Sam lengthened the chain, adding stretching, reading, and planning tasks.

The chain habit method gave Sam a tangible structure, turning overwhelming goals into bite-sized daily actions connected like dominos. This approach built resilience and a sense of mastery over time.

## Avoiding Common Pitfalls in Habit Change

Even with effective methods, habit change can stumble if common pitfalls aren't addressed. Awareness helps to anticipate and overcome them:

**Setting Unrealistic Goals:** Overambition leads to frustration and dropout. Start small and realistic to build confidence.

**Lack of Consistency:** Habits need repetition in stable contexts to form. Inconsistent practice weakens habit strength.

**Not Linking to Existing Routines:** Isolated new habits lack strong cues, making them easier to forget or skip.

**Ignoring Environmental Cues:** Environments supporting bad habits need modification to reduce triggers.

**Neglecting Progress Tracking:** Without feedback, motivation can fade. Tracking builds accountability and rewards.

**Expecting Immediate Results:** Habits often take weeks or months to become automatic. Patience supports perseverance.

**Overloading the Habit Chain:** Adding too many habits too fast causes overwhelm and failure. Slow incremental additions work better.

**Negative Self-Talk and Perfectionism:** Viewing slip-ups as failures can sabotage progress. Emphasize learning and resilience instead.

## Strategies to Avoid Pitfalls

Break goals into tiny, manageable pieces.

Anchor habits to strong, well-established cues.

Maintain a habit tracker or calendar.

Adjust the environment to minimize distractions and temptations.

Celebrate progress and forgive setbacks.

Gradually expand habit chains without rushing.

Seek support through accountability partners or communities.

The Chain Habit Method exploits the brain's craving for routine by linking habits into a smooth, automatic sequence. This approach lowers friction to habit formation and builds momentum, making change achievable and sustainable. Heartfelt stories like Sam's demonstrate how chaining tiny habits can transform an unfocused routine into structured growth.

Avoiding common pitfalls—unrealistic goals, inconsistency, neglecting cues, impatience—is crucial to maintaining progress and preventing discouragement. With conscious planning, patience, and kindness to yourself, you can effectively change habits and cultivate lasting improvement.

# Chapter Six

## Applying Tiny Habits in Key Areas of Life

**Health and Wellness: Small Steps to Big Gains**

Health and wellness form the foundation of a fulfilling life, yet many struggle with maintaining consistent, healthy routines. The key to sustainable improvement lies in the power of tiny habits — small, manageable changes that, when practiced regularly, accumulate into significant benefits over time.

Tiny habits are particularly effective in health because they require minimal effort initially, making barriers to starting very low. This approach bypasses the intimidation of big lifestyle overhauls and reduces the likelihood of failure and frustration. Just as brushing your teeth started as a conscious effort but eventually became automatic, tiny health habits can naturally integrate into your life with patience and persistence.

## Why Tiny Habits Work for Health

**Ease of Integration:** Tiny habits fit into existing routines, using natural cues for automatic practice—like drinking a glass of water after using the bathroom or stretching for a minute after waking up.

**Minimized Resistance:** Small actions reduce mental resistance and physical fatigue, boosting motivation and consistency.

**Compounding Impact:** Repeated small nutritious choices, brief exercises, or mindfulness sessions create lasting physiological and psychological benefits.

**Behavioral Momentum:** Early successes build confidence, encouraging larger and more frequent health-positive actions.

## Examples of Tiny Health Habits Making Big Gains

Drinking a glass of water first thing upon waking to hydrate and jumpstart metabolism.

Taking 5-minute mindful breathing or meditation breaks during hectic days to reduce stress and improve mental clarity.

Incorporating light stretching or brief walks every hour, especially for sedentary lifestyles, to promote circulation and reduce muscle stiffness.

Swapping sugary snacks with a handful of nuts or fresh fruit gradually improves nutrition without drastic dietary changes.

Using the stairs instead of the elevator a few times daily for a simple cardiovascular boost.

Laying out exercise clothes at night to ease morning workout initiation.

Practicing gratitude journaling as part of a bedtime routine to support emotional well-being and sleep quality.

Even the smallest lifestyle nudges, when consistently acted upon, lead to improvement in energy, mood, sleep, and chronic disease prevention over months and years.

## Lisa's Tiny Habit Health Turnaround

Lisa, a busy office worker and mother of two, always felt exhausted and out of shape. She wanted to make health changes but was overwhelmed by the idea of intensive workouts and dieting. After a health scare, she committed to tiny habits.

Starting with a single new action, Lisa placed a water bottle next to her bed and made a habit of finishing it each morning. This tiny practice improved her hydration, reducing morning fatigue. She then added two minutes of stretching after waking up, which gradually grew into a ten-minute yoga routine.

Lisa also shifted snack choices by keeping cut vegetables and fruits easily accessible at work. Over months, these effortless choices accumulated: more energy, better focus, and gradual weight loss. Lisa's story shows tiny health habits needn't be dramatic; they just need to be consistent.

## Practical Tips to Start Tiny Health Habits

Anchor habits to existing routines—take medicine after brushing teeth, walk after lunch.

Start with the smallest version, such as one push-up or a short walk.

Track progress visually—habit trackers or journals provide motivation.

Be patient with yourself and expect gradual results. Celebrate small victories.

Adjust environmental cues to support habits— prepare workout clothes, place healthy snacks in visible locations.

Partner with friends or family to build accountability and social support.

## The Science Behind Tiny Health Habits

Research reveals habits rely on cue-response-reward loops, and health behaviors are no exception. The "tiny" approach taps into this by breaking healthy behaviors into bite-sized actions, making them easier to repeat and less likely to trigger resistance or procrastination.

Studies show that even minimal physical activity— five minutes of walking every half hour—can significantly offset the harms of sedentary behavior. Likewise, hydration beginning with a single glass of water helps regulate many bodily functions, impacting cognition, mood, and energy.

Mindfulness and breathing exercises, even just five minutes daily, have been demonstrated to reduce cortisol levels and improve mental health. Thus, tiny shifts create ripples of benefit that extend beyond the initial action.

## Stress Reduction Through Mindful Habits

Stress manifests physically and emotionally as tension, irritability, or fatigue. While eliminating stressors completely may be impossible, cultivating mindful habits equips us to respond rather than react to stress.

Mindfulness—the practice of focusing on the present moment with acceptance—grounds tiny habits that interrupt stress spirals. Simple micro-practices such as deep breathing, sensory awareness, or brief meditations take only minutes but reset the nervous system effectively.

Examples include:

> Taking three slow, deep breaths before starting a task to calm racing thoughts.

> Performing a "5-4-3-2-1" grounding exercise: noticing 5 things seen, 4 things touched, 3 things heard, 2 things smelled, and 1 thing tasted to anchor in the present.

> Watching the flicker of a candle flame for a quiet moment of reflection.

Practicing mindful walking by paying attention to each step's sensation and rhythm.

Building mindful moments into daily routines, such as while waiting for coffee or brushing teeth, creates stress-reducing anchors throughout the day. These tiny habits reconnect mind and body, lowering cortisol levels and enhancing resilience.

## Enhancing Sleep Quality By Habit Adjustments

Good sleep is critical for health, yet many struggle with insomnia or poor sleep habits. Tiny habit adjustments around bedtime routines, environment, and mindset tackle sleep disorders gently and sustainably.

Effective tiny habits for better sleep include:

Setting a consistent bedtime by linking it to a relaxing cue like reading or light stretching.

Limiting screen time at least 30 minutes before sleep to reduce blue light exposure that inhibits melatonin production.

Drinking a small glass of water or herbal tea at a set time to signal winding down.

Incorporating brief gratitude journaling to shift the mind from worry to positivity.

Using calming scents like lavender or chamomile to create a soothing atmosphere.

These small changes improve circadian rhythm alignment, reduce sleep onset latency, and increase restorative sleep phases. The cumulative effect over weeks yields profound benefits in mood, cognitive function, and physical health.

## Emily's Path from Anxiety to Restful Nights

Emily, a high-stress professional, suffered from chronic insomnia exacerbated by anxiety. Nights were long and restless, impacting work and relationships. Traditional sleep hygiene advice felt overwhelming and hard to maintain consistently.

She discovered tiny habits focused on mindfulness and routine. Emily began with a simple practice: three slow breaths right after brushing her teeth before bed. This moment of calm became a signal for relaxation. She also introduced a five-minute gratitude journal, jotting down positive moments from the day, which shifted her focus away from worries.

Small environmental tweaks followed—dimming lights, using a lavender spray, and leaving phones outside the bedroom. These tiny habits took away the pressure of "fixing" sleep all at once, instead fostering a gentle, supportive nighttime ritual.

Within weeks, Emily noticed improved sleep onset and longer restorative sleep. Her anxiety lessened as mindful habits became part of her daily rhythm, showing how small, deliberate actions transform struggle into peaceful rest.

**Practical Tips for Implementing Tiny Habits for Stress and Sleep**

>Anchor mindful moments to daily routines like meals, commutes, or transitions.

>Start with extremely brief practices (1-3 minutes), building consistency first.

>Use physical cues — candlelight, water sips, or fragrance — to signal practice.

>Reduce screen exposure gradually; replace with relaxing activities like reading.

>Track progress lightly without pressure to reinforce habit formation.

>Be patient and compassionate with setbacks; habit building is non-linear.

Tiny habits, when thoughtfully applied, recalibrate stress responses and enhance sleep quality by fostering presence, relaxation, and environmental support. These small, consistent steps build a stable foundation for wellness that resonates beyond individual habits—nurturing mind, body, and spirit with lasting impact.

## Productivity Hacks Using Tiny Habits

In the quest for productivity, the answer isn't always to work harder or longer but to work smarter through tiny, consistent habits. These micro adjustments integrate easily into daily life, radically improving focus, efficiency, and overall output over time. Productivity isn't about grand gestures but the sum of deliberate small actions that build momentum effortlessly.

One of the most powerful tiny productivity hacks is the "two-minute rule." If a task takes less than two minutes—whether replying to an email, filing a document, or jotting down a to-do—it should be done immediately. This prevents minor tasks from piling up and reducing cognitive clutter. This simple rule instantly frees mental space and prevents overwhelm.

Another tiny habit is a five-minute declutter each morning. Clearing your workspace, organizing scattered papers, or closing unrelated tabs preps your environment for focus. It signals the brain that the day is ready for productive work and reduces distractions.

The Pomodoro Technique, a favorite for many, aligns with tiny habit philosophy by breaking work into focused 25-minute sprints followed by 5-minute breaks. Starting work in such small, manageable increments turns daunting projects into approachable chunks and sustains attention.

Mindful breaks are essential—taking 1-3 minutes to breathe deeply, stretch, or reflect rejuvenates your cognitive resources. Scheduling these mini pauses counteracts burnout while improving clarity and performance.

Prepping materials beforehand, known as the "20-second rule," lowers activation energy. Minimizing barriers to starting difficult or dreaded tasks increases likelihood of action. For example, laying out ingredients before cooking or opening a new file before work starts can transform inertia into flow.

Finally, focusing on a single task without multitasking preserves deep work capacity and quality. Tiny habits advocating task completion one at a time greatly enhance productivity.

## Relationships and Social Interaction Enhancements

Relationships are central to personal fulfillment and well-being. Yet, nurturing social ties often suffers due to busy lives or neglect of small consistent actions. Tiny habits bridge this gap by fostering connection with minimal time and effort.

Simple daily habits like sending a sincere message or compliment, remembering a birthday or special note, or actively listening create a ripple effect of appreciation and trust in relationships. These tiny behaviors, repeated consistently, deepen bonds beyond grand gestures.

Practicing active listening—summarizing or reflecting what a friend shared—demonstrates care and understanding. Integrating this into daily conversations helps avoid miscommunication and strengthens empathy.

Setting weekly micro-goals such as a short call with a family member or coffee with a colleague refreshes social networks gradually. Over time, these tiny social investments accumulate into meaningful relationships and support systems.

## Kevin's Productivity and Relationship Revival

Kevin, a software developer, felt drained professionally and lonely personally. Work stress lowered his output, and social isolation deepened his fatigue. Overwhelmed, Kevin began with tiny productivity habits: dedicating five minutes every morning to desk decluttering and applying the two-minute rule to small tasks like emails. These actions gave his workday structure and reduced stress.

Simultaneously, Kevin started a simple social habit: sending one genuine message daily to someone in his life. This tiny gesture led to rekindled friendships and new conversations filled with warmth and support.

Through these small, consistent shifts, Kevin revived his professional output and personal connections. Months later, his story illustrates that tiny habits, when layered thoughtfully, can transform complex challenges without pressure or burnout—balancing productivity with human connection.

# Chapter Seven

## Troubleshooting Habit Formation Challenges

### Identifying Barriers to Habit Success

Habit formation is a journey filled with opportunities for growth, but it is not without its obstacles. Even the most well-intentioned efforts toward building new habits can be hindered by various internal and external barriers. Recognizing these common roadblocks is the first crucial step toward overcoming them and creating sustainable, positive change.

This chapter explores the most frequent challenges individuals face when trying to establish habits, offering practical insights to identify and navigate these barriers compassionately and effectively. By understanding these obstacles, readers will gain tools to troubleshoot setbacks, maintain momentum, and achieve their habit goals.

## Common Barriers to Habit Success

### 1. Lack of Clear Goals

A frequent barrier to habit success is failure to set specific, measurable, and realistic goals. Vague intentions like "I want to exercise more" lack focus and direction, making it hard to measure progress or even start. Clear goals aligned with personal values and attainable within current circumstances foster stronger commitment.

### 2. Inadequate Planning and Preparation

Without a detailed plan connecting intentions to actions, habits are left to chance. Successful habit formation requires anticipating when, where, and how the behavior will occur. Techniques like "If-Then" planning ("If it's 7 AM, then I will go for a 5-minute walk") create concrete triggers and behavioral blueprints, minimizing uncertainty.

### 3. Overly Ambitious Expectations

Trying to change too much too soon often leads to burnout, discouragement, and abandonment of goals. Gradual progression through tiny, incremental steps lives at the heart of lasting change. Setting modest initial benchmarks boosts confidence and makes success feel achievable.

## 4. Environmental and Social Distractions

An unsupportive environment cluttered with competing stimuli distracts from habit formation. Physical clutter, frequent interruptions, internet distractions, or social pressures undermine focus and consistency. Modifying surroundings to reduce temptations and engaging social support systems empower habit success.

## 5. Procrastination and Lack of Motivation

Resistance to starting or continuing habits can stem from fear, overwhelm, or low energy. Breaking tasks into smaller components and connecting actions to meaningful "whys" reinforces motivation. Micro-habits take advantage of momentum, where the hardest part—starting—is minimized.

## 6. Forgetfulness and Disruptions in Routine

Life's unpredictability disrupts routines, leading to missed habit occurrences and fragility in habit strength. Forgetting is a natural cognitive limitation; using external reminders such as alarms or habit trackers provides effective support. Embracing a "never miss twice" mindset alleviates guilt and fosters resilience.

## 7. Negative Self-Talk and Perfectionism

Internal narratives that doubt ability or highlight

failures can derail effort. Viewing slip-ups as catastrophic rather than learning moments damages self-efficacy. Adopting a growth mindset—focusing on progress, not perfection—supports continued efforts despite setbacks.

## Maya's Battle with Habit Barriers

Maya had long dreamed of becoming more active but struggled to make exercise a lasting habit. Her goals were vague, her motivation inconsistent, and her busy schedule overwhelming. Early attempts to overhaul her routine with intense workouts ended in frustration and abandonment.

Through reflection, Maya identified her barriers: unrealistic expectations, lack of a clear plan, and distraction-filled environments. With support, she shifted to setting tiny, specific goals—walking for five minutes after breakfast—and created an "If-Then" plan anchored to existing habits.

She decluttered her workout space and enlisted her sister for accountability. When she missed days due to life's surprises, she reframed "failures" as temporary setbacks rather than defeats. Gradually, her confidence grew, and walking turned into longer, more frequent exercise.

Maya's journey demonstrates that barriers to habit success are common but surmountable with awareness, planning, external support, and self-compassion. Her story encourages persistence despite challenges.

## Strategies to Overcome Barriers

Set SMART goals (Specific, Measurable, Achievable, Relevant, Time-bound).

Develop "If-Then" action plans to anchor habits in consistent triggers.

Break goals into small, manageable steps and celebrate tiny wins.

Modify environments to eliminate distractions and cues for bad habits.

Use external prompts such as alarms, notes, or habit trackers.

Connect habits to personal values to strengthen motivation.

Seek social support or accountability partners.

Practice self-forgiveness and adjust goals flexibly based on experience.

Understanding these barriers equips habit changers to anticipate obstacles, troubleshoot effectively, and maintain steady progress. No journey toward better habits is linear, but with the right mindset and tools, setbacks become stepping stones instead of dead ends.

## Strategies for Staying Consistent Under Stress

Stress is an inevitable part of life, but it is also one of the greatest threats to forming and maintaining new habits. During stressful periods, the brain often defaults to habitual behaviors as coping mechanisms, which can mean reverting to old, unproductive patterns when new habits are most needed. Staying consistent under stress requires deliberate strategies to manage emotional triggers and preserve momentum.

One highly effective technique is **habit stacking**—linking a new habit to an existing, reliable routine. For example, attaching a brief mindfulness exercise to your morning coffee ritual creates a consistent anchor even on tough days. The familiarity of the cue lowers resistance and increases the likelihood of performance despite emotional turmoil.

**Mindfulness and deep breathing practices** serve as powerful stress reducers that can be micro-habits themselves. Taking just a few slow breaths or practicing 4-7-8 breathing activates the parasympathetic nervous system, calming the mind and reducing impulsive reactions that might derail habits.

Breaking tasks into **tiny, manageable steps** also reduces overwhelm. When stress amplifies the perceived difficulty of change, focusing on just the smallest action—like putting on workout shoes or writing a single sentence—makes starting easier and builds momentum.

Having a strong **support system** enhances resilience during stress. Sharing goals with friends or accountability partners provides encouragement and external motivation. Social reinforcement, even if just a quick check-in message, can be pivotal for staying on track.

Using **visual reminders and cues**—setting alarms, placing sticky notes, or habit-tracking apps—also compensates for memory lapses or decision fatigue that stress often induces.

Lastly, fostering **self-compassion** is crucial. Stressful moments inevitably bring slip-ups; treating yourself kindly and viewing setbacks as learning opportunities rather than failures preserves motivation and aids recovery.

## The Role of Environment in Habit Formation

The environment we inhabit profoundly shapes our habits because it provides the external cues that trigger behavior. Habit formation thrives when surroundings are designed to support desired actions and reduce obstacles.

An environment cluttered with distractions makes focus and repetition difficult. For instance, a messy workspace invites procrastination, while leaving workout clothes visible encourages physical activity. Environmental design leverages this by positioning cues strategically.

Physical cues can be manipulated to make good habits easy and bad habits hard. For example, placing a water bottle on your desk encourages hydration; conversely, removing junk food from the kitchen minimizes temptation.

Digital environments also impact habits. Reducing notifications, limiting tabs, or using apps to block distracting sites supports sustained attention.

Consistency benefits from establishing **dedicated spaces** for specific activities—like a reading nook or exercise area—where the context primes the brain for related behavior.

Social environment matters too. Surrounding yourself with people who reflect or support your goals exponentially increases success chances. Peer behaviors, group norms, and social accountability are powerful forces for habit adherence.

Ultimately, designing environments intentionally transforms the external world into a silent coach that guides behavior effortlessly, reducing reliance on willpower.

## Anna's Journey Through Stress and Environment Shift

Anna, a young professional, struggled to maintain healthy eating and exercise habits amid high work stress. During peak pressure periods, she defaulted to fast food and skipped workouts, feeling defeated and stuck.

She realized stress triggered her habit relapses and decided to apply tiny habit strategies to stay consistent. Anna began stacking a two-minute breathing exercise after her morning coffee to calm anxiety. She broke exercise into tiny steps, committing to just five-minute walks during breaks.

Crucially, she revamped her environment: cleared her kitchen of junk food and stocked easy-to-grab healthy snacks, moved her running shoes by the door, and created a small corner for yoga at home. Anna also enrolled her best friend as an accountability partner for joint workouts.

These changes not only made healthy habits easier but reduced the mental burden of choice. When stress came, Anna's environment and tiny habits sustained her progress.

Her story reveals how mindful management of stress and environment transforms habit formation from a daily battle into a supportive, nurturing process.

## Practical Tips for Navigating Stress and Environment

> Stack new habits on reliable daily routines to anchor consistent action under stress.

> Practice brief mindfulness or breathing exercises as part of habit routines.

> Start with micro habits during overwhelm to build momentum gradually.

Enlist support through social connections or accountability partners.

Use reminders—digital or physical—to cue habits and reinforce consistency.

Design spaces and digital environments to reduce friction for good habits and increase it for bad ones.

Be patient and compassionate during setbacks; focus on learning and restarting.

Consistency during difficult times depends on preparation, supportive contexts, and self-kindness. The environment you create and the strategies you apply determine whether stress becomes an obstacle or an opportunity for growth.

## How to Recover from Setbacks Effectively

Setbacks are an inevitable part of the habit formation journey. Whether missing days, slipping into old behaviors, or losing motivation temporarily, setbacks are not signs of failure but opportunities to learn and recalibrate. Recovering effectively requires a mindset rooted in self-compassion, reflection, and proactive planning.

The first key is to **accept setbacks without harsh self-criticism**. Viewing a missed day or lapse as a "failure" often triggers all-or-nothing thinking that leads to giving up entirely. Instead, adopt curiosity: What led to the setback? Were there triggers like stress, environment, or fatigue? What can be learned?

Once triggers are identified, create **actionable strategies to avoid or mitigate them**. For example, if skipping workouts happened due to busy schedules, design shorter, flexible versions of exercise routines that fit unpredictable days—a 5-minute stretch or walk instead of a full session.

**Reinforcing accountability** can reignite momentum. Sharing goals and setbacks with an accountability partner or group invites external motivation and support that buffers discouragement.

**Tracking progress visually**, like habit trackers or calendars, emphasizes the bigger picture—one setback does not erase accumulated progress. The motivation to maintain streaks encourages restarting promptly.

Setting **realistic expectations** is crucial. Habits are slowly cemented brain pathways and rarely formed linearly. Patience to persist through "messy middle" phases sustains progress.

Finally, practicing **self-kindness and resilience** heals emotional wounds setbacks may cause. Encouraging self-talk and celebrating small victories nurtures perseverance.

## When and How to Adjust Your Habit Plan

Rigidity in planning can stall progress when life situations or personal needs evolve. Habit plans should be living documents—adapted thoughtfully for sustained success.

Consider adjusting your habit plan when:

> Consistently missing habit occurrences or feeling overwhelmed

Finding previously motivating rewards less effective

Life circumstances change significantly (e.g., new job, family dynamics)

Physical or mental health demands shift

The habit no longer aligns with evolving values or goals

Effective adjustment requires honest evaluation: Are goals realistic? Are environmental supports adequate? Is the habit meaningful?

Modifications can include:

**Scaling down intensity or frequency:** A daily 30-minute workout might shift to 10 minutes on busy days.

**Changing habit triggers:** If morning habits fail, try evening anchors instead.

**Altering the habit itself while preserving the reward:** Swap jogging for cycling if joint pain occurs but maintain the health benefit.

**Adding social or accountability elements:** Joining groups or involving partners for motivation.

**Refining plans based on data:** Use habit tracking visuals and journals to spot trends and inform tweaks.

Adjustments should focus on maintaining momentum through achievable, relevant, and enjoyable actions rather than punishment for perceived "failures."

## David's Journey Back from Setbacks

David, a software engineer, struggled with establishing a morning exercise habit. Initial enthusiasm saw consistent workouts for months, but a demanding project led to missed sessions, guilt, and eventual abandonment.

Frustrated and discouraged, David reflected on what caused the setback. He noticed fatigue and unrealistic expectations triggered his lapse. Instead of giving up, David adjusted by downsizing his routine to 5-minute energizing stretches on tough days. He also moved from early mornings to midday breaks when he felt more alert.

David used a habit tracker app to visualize his progress and shared his goals with a friend who checked in regularly. This external accountability, combined with flexible planning and self-kindness, rekindled David's habit.

Over time, David rebuilt consistency with a habit plan that matched his reality—showing that setbacks don't define trajectory but reveal paths to better strategies and resilience.

## Practical Tips for Setback Recovery and Plan Adjustment

- Normalize setbacks as opportunities for learning, not failure.

- Practice gentle self-talk and curiosity over criticism.

- Analyze setback triggers and design manageable alternative strategies.

- Use habit trackers and accountability systems to maintain motivation.

Regularly review and adjust habit goals, triggers, and rewards.

Embrace flexibility in routine timing, duration, and format.

Connect habits closely to personal values to sustain meaning.

Celebrate small wins to nourish perseverance.

Habits form and evolve within complex life contexts. Recovering from setbacks and skillfully adjusting plans are essential competencies along the path to lasting change. This chapter section provides a compassionate, practical framework to navigate these challenges effectively.

# Chapter Eight

## Making Tiny Habits Stick for a Lifetime

Creating a Personalized Habit System

Making tiny habits stick is not merely about starting new routines but about embedding them deeply into the fabric of your unique life. A one-size-fits-all approach rarely succeeds because individuals differ in their environments, personalities, motivations, and challenges. Creating a personalized habit system tailors habit formation to your specific context, maximizing relevance, feasibility, and sustainability.

This chapter guides you through designing a custom habit system—one that integrates seamlessly into your daily rhythms, aligns with your values, honors your natural tendencies, and remains flexible to evolve with your life. By doing so, habits become part of your identity, not just isolated actions.

## Why Personalization Matters

Scientific research and real-world experience show that habits formed in direct response to individual needs and contexts are more resilient. Personalized habit systems minimize friction and enhance motivation by leveraging intrinsic rewards and natural incentives unique to you.

For example, a morning exercise habit is likely to stick better if it fits your energy peaks, preferred workout type, and home setup. Similarly, a habit linked to meaningful values or social roles—like journaling to enhance self-awareness—fosters deeper commitment.

## Steps to Create Your Personalized Habit System

### 1. Identify Meaningful Goals and Values
Reflect on what matters most in your life—health, creativity, relationships, career, or peace of mind. Connect habits to these core drivers to cultivate motivation beyond external pressures.

### 2. Analyze Your Current Routines and Triggers
Map out daily activities where habits could naturally anchor. Look for stable cues like brushing teeth,

morning coffee, or commuting moments. Habit stacking or chaining maximizes responsiveness.

### 3. Start Tiny and Specific
Determine the smallest habit unit possible—a single push-up, one paragraph writing, drinking one glass of water. Clear specificity reduces ambiguity and decision paralysis.

### 4. Leverage Technology and Tools
Use habit trackers, reminders, or apps customized to your preferences. Visual progress and regular nudges sustain momentum.

### 5. Incorporate Flexibility and Adaptation
Build buffer days or alternative habits for busy or low-energy times. Periodically review and adjust your system to keep it aligned and sustainable.

### 6. Build Social and Environmental Supports
Inform family or friends of goals, enlist accountability partners, and optimize your surroundings to cue and reward habits.

### 7. Celebrate and Reflect
Regularly acknowledge your progress and reflect on insights gained to reinforce learning and resilience.

## Alex's Personalized Habit System Transformation

Alex, a busy professional and parent, struggled with inconsistent habits due to a hectic, unpredictable schedule. She often started ambitious routines but found them incompatible with personal and family rhythms.

With guidance, Alex created a personalized habit system focusing on micro goals aligned with her priorities: morning hydration linked to waking up, evening gratitude journaling as part of bedtime, and 5-minute midday stretches during work breaks.

She adopted technology—a simple habit tracker app—to monitor consistency and visualize progress. Alex involved her partner to share goals and encourage each other, creating accountability and emotional support.

Crucially, Alex allowed herself flexibility. On hectic days, she did only the smallest version of habits, avoiding overwhelm without losing continuity. Monthly reflections helped her tweak routines to fit evolving demands.

Over time, these personalized habits not only grounded Alex's days but reshaped her identity into "someone who cares for her health and well-being," leading to natural, sustained habit adherence.

## Practical Tips for Designing Your Habit System

Spend time reflecting on what you truly want and why it matters to YOU.

Choose cues embedded in daily life for habit attachment.

Start so small that saying yes feels natural and effortless.

Use apps or journals that suit your style for tracking progress.

Recruit friends or family members to support and cheer your journey.

Embrace setbacks and adjust habits without guilt or haste.

Celebrate even minor wins to sustain enthusiasm and confidence.

Making tiny habits stick is a lifelong journey that requires mindset, strategy, and self-awareness. Creating a personalized system empowers habits to become effortless extensions of your life, producing lasting transformation with joy and ease.

## Celebrating Milestones to Build Commitment

Celebrating milestones is a vital, often underestimated element in building long-lasting habits. Milestones—whether small daily wins or significant achievements—serve as markers of progress and affirm the value of persistent effort. When intentionally acknowledged, milestones provide motivation, boost self-confidence, and deepen emotional investment in the habit formation journey.

Celebrations don't require grandeur or expense; even simple recognition can have profound effects. This could be mentally appreciating your commitment after a week of consistency or rewarding yourself with a favorite treat or activity after reaching a specific goal. Such acts create positive associations with the habit, reinforcing the cue-routine-reward cycle essential for durability.

Reflecting on milestones helps maintain perspective. In moments of frustration or doubt, revisiting progress counters negative thoughts and fosters resilience. Visual tools like milestone jars—where you write down each success and revisit whenever needed—strengthen this effect by making achievements tangible.

Celebrating also combats burnout by injecting joy into the process. Recognizing hard work validates effort beyond outcomes and nurtures a growth mindset where progress, not perfection, is the goal.

**Examples of Celebrating Milestones**

After completing a month of regular exercise, allow yourself a small indulgence like a massage or special meal.

Mark a streak of productive workdays with a social event or outing with friends.

Celebrate learning a new skill by sharing your achievement with supportive peers.

Keep a journal or jar of milestones to review on challenging days, reminding you of your growth.

Pause to enjoy simple pleasures after daily accomplishments, such as a favorite music track or nature walk.

These celebratory touches reinforce habit loops and transform effort into sustained commitment.

## Using Rewards and Accountability Partners

Rewards and accountability partners are powerful social and psychological tools that bolster habit formation. Rewards provide immediate gratification and positive reinforcement, essential in the often slow, gradual process of habit crystallization. Accountability partners add external motivation, encouragement, and a sense of obligation that heightens consistency.

**Effective reward systems** align with personal values and do not undermine habit goals. For example, a non-food reward for healthy eating—like a new workout outfit or a leisure outing—maintains congruence. Rewards should feel meaningful but not so large that they create pressure or dependency.

**Accountability partners** hold you responsible, celebrate wins with you, and provide support during setbacks. This can be a friend, family member, colleague, or coach. Sharing goals publicly, setting check-in times, or joining group challenges leverages social bonds to fuel adherence.

The combined use of rewards and accountability typically produces stronger habit maintenance than internal motivation alone, especially when motivation fluctuates.

## Maya's Journey of Commitment and Support

Maya, a new mother and graduate student, wanted to integrate daily meditation into her chaotic life but struggled with consistency and self-doubt. Her progress was slow, and discouragement mounted quickly.

Her mentor suggested celebrating every five-day streak with a small ritual—a hot bath or favorite snack—to make achieving milestones enjoyable. Maya also partnered with a friend to check in each morning, fostering accountability and shared encouragement.

The combination of milestones celebrations and social accountability transformed Maya's journey. The positive experiences associated with milestones made meditation something she looked forward to. Sharing progress with her friend kept her motivated even on the hardest days.

Maya's path reveals that commitment flourishes when nurtured with kindness, celebration, and connection—ingredients that make tiny habits stick for a lifetime.

## Practical Tips for Celebrations, Rewards, and Accountability

Break big goals into smaller milestones to celebrate frequently.

Choose personalized rewards that support habit goals rather than contradict them.

Use visual progress tools like streak trackers or milestone jars.

Select accountability partners who are genuinely supportive and proactive.

Schedule regular check-ins to maintain responsibility.

Celebrate publicly when comfortable to amplify motivation.

Reflect on setbacks later while focusing celebrations on progress.

Celebrating milestones, using rewards thoughtfully, and embracing accountability partners collectively build a robust habit system aligned for enduring success. They transform habit formation from a solitary struggle into a shared, joyful journey.

## Long-Term Benefits of Habit Mastery

Mastering tiny habits is much more than just automating small actions; it transforms the foundation of daily life and personality over the long haul. Habit mastery shapes behavior patterns, emotional regulation, cognitive function, and overall well-being in profound ways.

Long-term habit mastery offers these key benefits:

**Automaticity reduces decision fatigue:** When healthy, productive habits become automatic, mental energy is preserved for complex decisions. This increases efficiency and reduces burnout.

**Neural rewiring and lasting brain changes:** Repeated habits strengthen neural pathways, embedding behavior deeply. This neurological shift makes positive behaviors effortless and resilient against stress or disruption.

**Sustained motivation and confidence:** Success in forming and maintaining habits boosts self-efficacy—a powerful predictor of future goal achievement. Confidence grows, making subsequent habits easier to build.

**Cumulative improvements in health and performance:** Incremental positive behaviors compound to produce outsized benefits in fitness, cognitive clarity, emotional stability, and social connection.

**Identity transformation:** Over time, consistent habits become part of your self-concept. You shift identity from "someone who tries" to "someone who follows through," increasing alignment between actions and values.

Real-life habit mastery creates a virtuous cycle where improved behavior breeds better outcomes, which then reinforce commitment to habits. This momentum fuels continuing growth in multiple life areas.

## Embracing a Growth Mindset for Continuous Change

A growth mindset—the belief that abilities and traits can develop with effort and learning—is vital for maintaining momentum in lifelong habit formation. Habit mastery is not a one-time achievement but an evolving process marked by constant refinement and adaptation.

With a growth mindset:

Setbacks and failures aren't permanent markers but learning opportunities that illuminate paths forward.

New challenges become exciting prospects for growth rather than threats to identity.

Feedback—whether internal or external—is embraced as valuable information rather than criticism.

Persistence is fueled by the understanding that change requires time and practice.

Self-compassion tempers frustration, making habit journeys sustainable through highs and lows.

Adopting a growth mindset shifts the focus from proving competence to cultivating competence, nurturing resilience and joy in progress.

## Elysia's Journey from Struggle to Mastery

Elysia had long struggled to maintain an exercise routine, cycling through enthusiasm and relapse. Early failures on her fitness journey eroded confidence and spawned self-doubt.

Upon learning about habit science and adopting a growth mindset, Elysia redefined her approach. She set tiny, specific habits—to wear workout clothes immediately after waking and do just five minutes of stretching. Celebrating these micro wins connected her habit to her identity as a healthy person.

Elysia viewed setbacks as experiments, valuable information guiding her refinements. When tired or busy, she adapted the routine rather than abandoning it, prioritizing consistency over intensity. Internalizing that mastery is a journey, not a destination, helped her balance ambition with kindness to herself.

Over months, Elysia's tiny habits rewired her brain, transformed her self-image, and boosted her emotional resilience. Her story reveals that habit mastery powered by a growth mindset creates lasting, meaningful change.

## Practical Advice to Cultivate Habit Mastery and Growth Mindset

Focus on mastering one tiny habit at a time, ensuring completeness before adding new ones.

Regularly reflect on progress with curiosity, embracing setbacks as teachers.

Reframe challenges as opportunities to learn and grow.

Celebrate incremental successes to build motivation and confidence.

Develop self-compassion to weather inevitable fluctuations without giving up.

Foster a learning orientation: stay curious about what habit science reveals.

Align habits with personal values to enhance meaning and persistence.

Habit mastery and a growth mindset form the twin pillars of sustainable behavior change. Together, they empower tiny habits not merely to stick but to flourish, enabling continuous evolution and thriving in life's complexities.

# Conclusion

The Power and Promise of Tiny Habits for Lifelong Change

This book has explored the transformative power of tiny habits—small, manageable actions integrated thoughtfully into daily life—and how they catalyze sustained personal growth across health, productivity, relationships, and mindset. Embracing tiny habits represents a seismic shift away from the often overwhelming pursuit of massive changes and rigid discipline, replacing it with ease, grace, and steady momentum.

At the heart of effective habit change is the understanding that behavior does not rely solely on motivation or willpower, which tend to fluctuate unpredictably. Instead, success hinges on creating systems that align habits with existing routines, clear cues, manageable abilities, and immediate rewards. This aligns with the Fogg Behavior Model— where Motivation, Ability, and Prompt interact— illustrating why the tiniest positive actions yield outsized results when designed well.

As you have seen throughout this book, the journey of habit mastery is profoundly human—a blend of science, psychology, trial, error, and compassion. The heart-to-heart stories threaded into each chapter remind us that setbacks are normal and no one's journey is perfect or linear. Rather, resilience, adaptability, and kindness toward ourselves magnify our potential for lasting transformation.

Celebrating milestones fosters emotional connection to the process and reinforces momentum, while rewards and accountability partners anchor external motivation and social reinforcement. Designing personalized habit systems empowers you to tailor change efforts to your unique life context, making new behaviors congruent with your values, rhythms, and challenges.

The long-term benefits of habit mastery ripple beyond immediate habit outcomes. They replenish mental energy by reducing decision fatigue, strengthen neural pathways supporting automatic good behavior, improve self-confidence, and ultimately reshape identity. When habits become part of who you are, growth becomes not just possible but joyful and natural.

Embracing a growth mindset provides the soil for continuous improvement and learning. Viewing challenges as opportunities, mistakes as lessons, and effort as cultivation helps sustain progress through ups and downs. Change, then, becomes a lifelong adventure rather than a deadline to reach or a scoreboard to win.

This comprehensive approach to tiny habits, supported by scientific evidence and enriched with lived experiences, offers a holistic roadmap to sustainable improvement. Whether you aim to enhance health, build productivity, nurture relationships, or evolve mentally and emotionally, starting tiny creates a foundation upon which to build extraordinary lives.

The power to change resides within small, consistent steps—anchored in your daily reality and nurtured with patience and kindness. With this knowledge, you are equipped not just to form habits but to transform life itself.

Go forth with courage and curiosity. Your tiny habits today are the architects of your resilient, vibrant tomorrow.